# INTRODUCTION TO OUR REVISION GUIDE

- The content of all the major specifications has been distilled to the essentials in this guide to provide you with a set of user-friendly and well organised revision notes in full colour.

- All you need for the exam is here, but don't just read! **LEARN ACTIVELY!**

- Constantly test yourself, without looking at the book.

- When you have revised a section or a diagram, **PLACE A BOLD TICK AGAINST IT.** Similarly, tick the "Progress and Revision" section of the contents when you have done a page. This is great for your self confidence.

- Many questions depend only on straightforward recall of facts, so make sure you learn them!

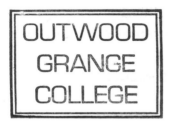

OUTWOOD
GRANGE
COLLEGE

**IMPORTANT POINT:** Energy is often referred to as being "used". In this guide for greater scientific accuracy we refer to it being "transferred" into other forms.

**CONSULTANT EDITORS ...**
**CLARE TOWNSEND**
**DAVID CHARLES**

Many thanks to the **HUDDERSFIELD EXAMINER** for allowing us to reproduce action photographs from their archives and in particular to Lynda Thwaites for helping us to select them.

- Thanks also to Barry Adams for taking the pupil photographs

# CONTENTS

# • CONTENTS

## Definitions Of Health And Fitness

### HEALTH

'A state of complete PHYSICAL, MENTAL and SOCIAL WELL BEING'.

PHYSICALLY, all my body systems are working well, and I have no illness or injuries.

MENTALLY, I feel good about myself, my emotions are under control and I don't feel stressed.

SOCIALLY, I have all the basic necessities of life, the support of friends, and an awareness of my role in society.

### FITNESS

'The ability to meet the demands of your ENVIRONMENT and LIFESTYLE' and still have energy left for emergencies

School and home form my immediate ENVIRONMENT and they present me with certain responsibilities which I must face up to on a daily basis.

My LIFESTYLE also places demands on me e.g. sport at school, my part-time job on Sundays, and partying on Saturday night!

Because I'm reasonably fit, I cope with my life with energy to spare.

PHYSICAL EXERCISE is the key which links HEALTH and FITNESS.

HEALTH — PHYSICAL EXERCISE — FITNESS

LIFELONG EXERCISE is the key to LIFELONG HEALTH.

## Physical Fitness And Motor Fitness

### 1. GENERAL FITNESS

- This is sometimes called health-related fitness because it relates to the type of fitness required by a normal person to cope with the daily demands made of them.

- The five components vary in their necessity from person to person. Fitness is relative and is specific to your own environment. A person working at a desk in an office would not necessarily need to be as physically fit as someone labouring on a building site. They may need to be mentally more fit, however.

STRENGTH | SUPPLENESS | STAMINA | SPEED | SOMATOTYPE — GENERAL FITNESS

### 2. MOTOR FITNESS

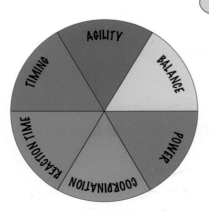

AGILITY, BALANCE, POWER, COORDINATION, REACTION TIME, TIMING

| | | |
|---|---|---|
| AGILITY | - | being able to alter your position and direction at speed. |
| BALANCE | - | maintaining the correct position without faltering during the execution of your performance. |
| POWER | - | being able to transfer energy at speed i.e. explosive strength. |
| COORDINATION | - | being able to synchronise the movements of different body parts in response to the task. |
| TIMING | - | acting at precisely the correct moment. |
| REACTION TIME | - | the time it takes to react i.e. your speed of thought and action. |

## The Skeleton

The skeleton gives the body its shape. It is made up of 206 bones in total, which come in FOUR types, LONG BONES, SHORT BONES, FLAT BONES and IRREGULAR BONES. These are held together by joints.

### PROTECTION

Parts of the body are delicate and could be easily damaged. The skeleton protects them. The most delicate part of the body is the BRAIN which is protected by the CRANIUM. The SPINAL CORD, which runs down the back of the body is protected by the VERTEBRAE. Your RIBS and STERNUM protect the HEART and LUNGS. Altogether your RIBS form an expandible cage called the RIB CAGE.

### BLOOD FORMATION

Inside the larger bones of the body bone marrow produces red blood cells. Areas where this takes place include the HUMERUS, RIBS and the FEMUR

BONE MARROW

### MOVEMENT

Some of the bones of the body are held together by freely moveable joints. This means you are able to bend your body and move about.

### SUPPORT

The skeleton gives the body its shape, otherwise it would be flabby and shapeless!
It also holds your vital organs in place, by providing a framework.

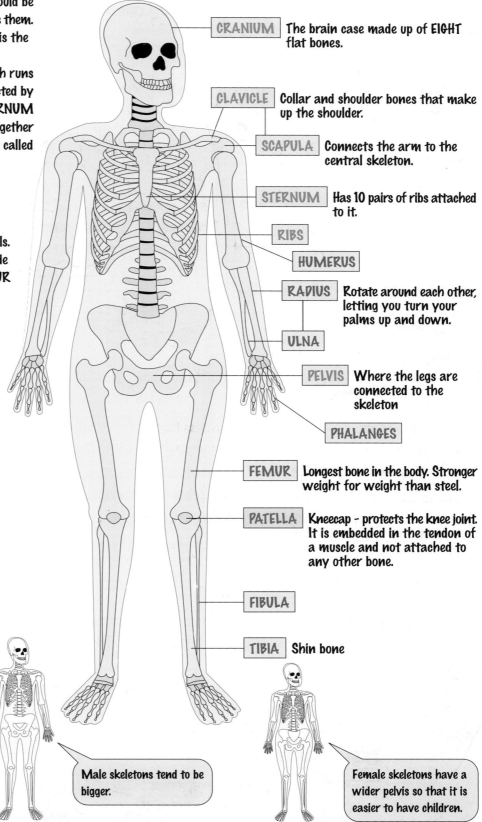

CRANIUM — The brain case made up of EIGHT flat bones.

CLAVICLE — Collar and shoulder bones that make up the shoulder.

SCAPULA — Connects the arm to the central skeleton.

STERNUM — Has 10 pairs of ribs attached to it.

RIBS

HUMERUS

RADIUS — Rotate around each other, letting you turn your palms up and down.

ULNA

PELVIS — Where the legs are connected to the skeleton

PHALANGES

FEMUR — Longest bone in the body. Stronger weight for weight than steel.

PATELLA — Kneecap - protects the knee joint. It is embedded in the tendon of a muscle and not attached to any other bone.

FIBULA

TIBIA — Shin bone

Male skeletons tend to be bigger.

Female skeletons have a wider pelvis so that it is easier to have children.

○ FLAT BONES
○ LONG BONES
○ SHORT BONES
○ IRREGULAR BONES

## The Vertebral Column

The vertebral column has **3** main functions ...

- ... SUPPORT. It is literally the "backbone" of the body and as such transfers the weight of the body downwards to the pelvis.
- ... MOVEMENT. Even though the individual vertebrae are held together by slightly moveable joints, the presence of so many of them allows great flexibility.
- ... PROTECTION. The spinal cord, a bundle of nerves relaying information to and from the brain, runs through and is protected by the vertebral column.

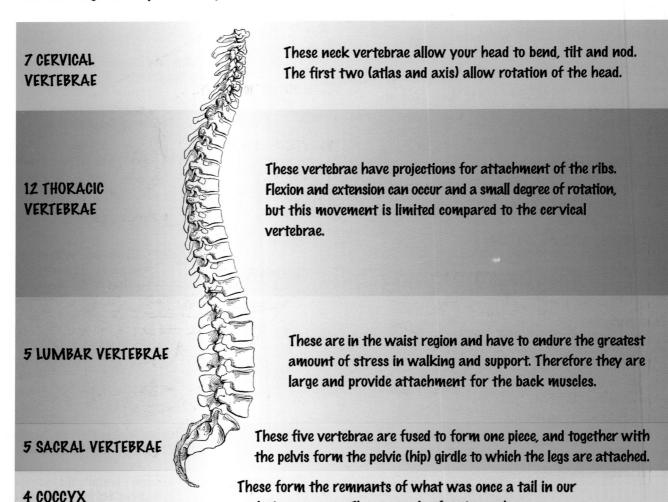

**7 CERVICAL VERTEBRAE**
These neck vertebrae allow your head to bend, tilt and nod. The first two (atlas and axis) allow rotation of the head.

**12 THORACIC VERTEBRAE**
These vertebrae have projections for attachment of the ribs. Flexion and extension can occur and a small degree of rotation, but this movement is limited compared to the cervical vertebrae.

**5 LUMBAR VERTEBRAE**
These are in the waist region and have to endure the greatest amount of stress in walking and support. Therefore they are large and provide attachment for the back muscles.

**5 SACRAL VERTEBRAE**
These five vertebrae are fused to form one piece, and together with the pelvis form the pelvic (hip) girdle to which the legs are attached.

**4 COCCYX**
These form the remnants of what was once a tail in our evolutionary past. These are also fused together.

## Joining Bones To Bones

- Where two bones meet, the surfaces rub against one another as movement occurs. To reduce the amount of friction, a layer of SMOOTH CARTILAGE covers the ends.

- In the vertebral column, the cartilage forms discs which act as shock absorbers between each individual vertebrae.

- In SYNOVIAL JOINTS, friction is also reduced by a thin layer of lubricating liquid called SYNOVIAL FLUID (see next page).

- Holding the bones together are tough, fibrous straps called LIGAMENTS. These are reasonably elastic to allow movement at the joint.

## Immovable (Fixed) Joints

- These occur where movement would be a severe disadvantage e.g. the bones of the cranium, the joint between the pelvis and the vertebral column.
- The joints are held together by tough, fibrous tissue which develops during childhood.

## Slightly Moveable Joints

- Here, movement is needed but only to a certain point e.g. the vertebral column.
- Individual vertebrae are separated by cartilage and held together by tough, fibrous bands called ligaments (see previous page).

## Freely Moveable Joints

These are also called SYNOVIAL joints, and occur in most places in the body where a reasonable degree of movement occurs.

- Characteristically they are surrounded by a CAPSULE, the internal lining of which secretes SYNOVIAL FLUID to LUBRICATE the joint.

○ TOUGH OUTER LIGAMENTS
● CAPSULE OF THE JOINT
● SYNOVIAL MEMBRANE
○ SYNOVIAL FLUID
○ CARTILAGE

A Synovial Joint

## Types Of Freely Moveable Joint

### BALL AND SOCKET JOINT

e.g. The hip and shoulder joints

ALLOWS A FULL RANGE OF MOVEMENT

### PIVOT JOINT

ALLOWS ROTATION

e.g. Atlas and axis in the neck

### HINGE JOINT

MOVEMENT IN ONE PLANE: FLEXION AND EXTENSION

e.g. The elbow and knee joints

### SADDLE JOINT

e.g. Thumb

TIGHT-FITTING SURFACES MOVE SIDE TO SIDE + FORWARDS + BACK

### CONDYLOID JOINT

e.g. Wrist

### GLIDING JOINTS

These occur in the many small bones of the hands and feet. They allow a slight sliding motion forwards and backwards and from side to side.

## Types Of Movement In Relation To Physical Activities

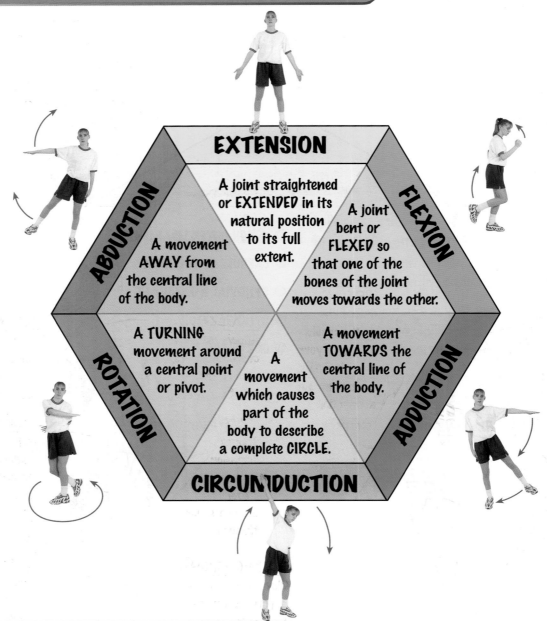

**EXTENSION**
A joint straightened or EXTENDED in its natural position to its full extent.

**FLEXION**
A joint bent or FLEXED so that one of the bones of the joint moves towards the other.

**ABDUCTION**
A movement AWAY from the central line of the body.

**ROTATION**
A TURNING movement around a central point or pivot.

A movement which causes part of the body to describe a complete CIRCLE.

**ADDUCTION**
A movement TOWARDS the central line of the body.

**CIRCUMDUCTION**

## Joints That Can Perform These Movements

|  | HINGE | BALL AND SOCKET | PIVOT | CONDYLOID | SADDLE | GLIDING |
|---|---|---|---|---|---|---|
| FLEXION | ✓ | ✓ |  | ✓ | ✓ | A SMALL AMOUNT OF THESE TYPES OF MOVEMENT |
| EXTENSION | ✓ | ✓ |  | ✓ | ✓ | |
| ABDUCTION |  | ✓ |  | ✓ | ✓ | |
| ADDUCTION |  | ✓ |  | ✓ | ✓ | |
| ROTATION |  | ✓ | ✓ |  |  | |
| CIRCUMDUCTION |  | ✓ |  |  |  | |

Every movement of your body depends on muscles.
These are three different types of muscle.

## 1. INVOLUNTARY (Smooth)

- Found mainly surrounding hollow organs e.g. blood vessels, gut.
- Performs its function without any conscious control, but usually quite slowly.

## 2. VOLUNTARY (Skeletal)

- Found mainly attached to the skeleton.
- Capable of rapid contraction which causes skeletal movement.
- Under conscious control e.g. all conscious movement.

## 3. CARDIAC

- Found only in the walls of the heart.
- Undergoes constant automatic rhythmical contractions.
- No conscious control.

## Voluntary Muscles – How They Perform In Detail

### FRONT

**PECTORALS**
Create adduction at the shoulder across the chest, e.g. press-ups.

**ABDOMINALS**
Allow you to flex your trunk, e.g. sit-ups.

**QUADRICEPS**
Makes extension of the leg possible at the knee, e.g. squats, kicking.

**DELTOIDS**
Create abduction at the shoulder and raise your arm sideways, e.g. swimming arm action.

**BICEPS**
Allows flexion at the elbow, e.g. chin-ups.

### BACK

**TRAPEZIUS**
Allows rotation of the shoulders, e.g. cricket bowling action.

**TRICEPS**
Creates extension at the elbow. e.g. press-ups, throwing.

**GASTROCNEMIUS**
Allows you to stand on your tiptoes, by creating extension at the ankle, e.g. sprinting (start).

**LATISSIMUS**
Adduction at the shoulder behind your back, e.g. rope climb.

**GLUTEALS**
Allow extension, abduction and adduction at the hip. (Gluteus Maximus is the biggest Gluteal). e.g. squats, jumping.

**HAMSTRINGS**
These allow flexion of the leg at the knee, e.g. sprinting (leg action recovery).

## Muscle Attachment

ORIGIN

INSERTION

Voluntary muscles are attached to your skeleton by TENDONS , usually across a synovial joint. These are fibrous and INELASTIC.

**A** The point where the muscle tendon attaches to the fixed or stationary bone is called the ORIGIN.

**B** The point where the muscle tendon attaches to the moving bone is called the INSERTION.

As muscles contract they shorten. This makes the joint move.

**WHEN A MUSCLE CONTRACTS THE INSERTION MOVES TOWARDS THE ORIGIN.**

Muscles can only create movement in ONE direction ... by becoming SHORTER!!

This means you need TWO muscles at every joint to allow movement in TWO directions.

SO MUSCLES WORK IN PAIRS.

WHEN YOUR BICEPS CONTRACT IT MAKES YOUR ELBOW FLEX, PULLING YOUR FOREARM UP.

TO ALLOW YOUR ELBOW TO EXTEND, YOU NEED YOUR TRICEPS TO CONTRACT AND PULL YOUR ARM BACK DOWN. (OR RELY ON GRAVITY!)

Muscles working in opposite directions like this are said to be working ANTAGONISTICALLY.
The muscle doing the work and creating the movement is called the AGONIST or PRIME MOVER.
The muscle which is relaxing and letting the movement take place, is called the ANTAGONIST.

So, in the example of the arm, when you flex your elbow, e.g. during a bicep curl
the bicep is the AGONIST
and the tricep is the ANTAGONIST.

AGONIST

ANTAGONIST

When other muscles ASSIST the PRIME MOVER in creating
a movement, these other muscles are called SYNERGISTS. e.g. deltoids doing press-ups

## Types Of Muscle Contraction

### 1. ISOMETRIC CONTRACTION

- Here, the muscle stays the SAME LENGTH as it works and so no movement occurs.

- The muscles in the vertebral column contract isometrically to maintain our posture.

### 2. ISOTONIC CONTRACTION

- Here, the muscle CHANGES ITS LENGTH as it works ...

- Shortening is called CONCENTRIC CONTRACTION, and lengthening under tension is called ECCENTRIC CONTRACTION.

All muscles have fast and slow twitch fibres or a mixture of the two. The proportions are inherited.

### FAST TWITCH FIBRES

- Produce POWERFUL contractions VERY QUICKLY (EXPLOSIVE).

- These fibres become FATIGUED in a short time.

- Great for sprinting and fast bowling.

### SLOW TWITCH FIBRES

- Produce less powerful, slower contractions.

- Become fatigued less quickly.

- Ideal for endurance events. e.g. marathon running.

## The Function Of The Circulatory System

The circulatory system is the body's transport system.
- It carries blood from the heart to all the cells of the body ...
- ... to provide them with FOOD and OXYGEN, and ...
- ... carries WASTE PRODUCTS including CARBON DIOXIDE away from the cells.
- Blood is pumped to the lungs so that OXYGEN and CARBON DIOXIDE can be exchanged.
- The system consists of THE HEART , THE BLOOD VESSELS , and THE BLOOD.

LUNGS
® ⓛ
HEART
BODY

■ = DEOXYGENATED
■ = OXYGENATED

## The Heart And Major Blood Vessels

The heart acts as a PUMP in a DOUBLE CIRCULATORY SYSTEM.

- As you can see blood flows around a 'figure of eight' circuit and passes through the heart TWICE on each circuit.
- Blood travels AWAY from the heart through ARTERIES, ...
- ... and returns to the heart through VEINS.

There are TWO SEPARATE CIRCULATION SYSTEMS, ...

One 'loop' carries blood from the HEART to the LUNGS and then back to the HEART ...

... and the other carries blood from the HEART to ALL OTHER PARTS OF THE BODY and then back to the HEART.

The RIGHT SIDE of the heart pumps blood which is LOW IN OXYGEN to the LUNGS, to pick up OXYGEN.

The LEFT SIDE of the heart pumps blood which is RICH IN OXYGEN to all other parts of the BODY.

■ Blood low in oxygen (DEOXYGENATED)
■ Blood rich in oxygen (OXYGENATED)

## How The Heart Pumps Blood

For substances to be delivered and removed from the cells efficiently, the blood must flow at an appropriate rate. The regular contracting and relaxing of the heart ensures this ...

- During RELAXATION PHASE, blood flows into the heart from the lungs and body.
- The upper chambers then squeeze blood into the lower chambers.

- During CONTRACTION PHASE, the lower chambers contract forcing blood to the body and lungs.
- The cycle then starts again.

## The Three Types Of Blood Vessel

- Thick, elastic wall to cope with high pressure ...
- ... of blood expelled from the heart.
- Rich in OXYGEN and FOOD.

ARTERY — VEIN

A CAPILLARY NETWORK IN A MUSCLE.

CAPILLARY

- Thinner, less elastic walls ...
- ... containing valves to ...
- ... prevent backflow of blood on the way back to the heart.
- Rich in CARBON DIOXIDE and WASTE.

- Narrow, thin-walled vessels ...
- ... just one cell thick.

## Exchange Of Substances At The Capillaries

The heart and blood vessels provide a route around the body, but it is the BLOOD which actually TRANSPORTS substances. Exchange of substances between the blood and the body tissues can ONLY OCCUR IN CAPILLARIES. Substances diffuse from the blood into the cells and vice versa. The cells exchange carbon dioxide and waste for oxygen and food.

- Food (e.g. glucose) from the digestive system or the liver is carried in the plasma.
- Oxygen from the lungs is carried by the Red Blood Cells.

MUSCLE CELLS

WASTE — CARBON DIOXIDE — OXYGEN — FOOD

A CAPILLARY VESSEL (one cell thick)

- Waste from the cells is carried in the plasma.
- Carbon dioxide from respiration in the cells is carried in the plasma.

## The Blood

If blood is allowed to stand without clotting, it separates out into its 4 components ...

PLASMA is a straw-coloured liquid which transports
- ... Carbon dioxide from the cells to the lungs ...
- ... Glucose from the small intestine to the cells ...
- ... wastes (e.g. Urea) from the cells.

WHITE CELLS have a nucleus which is variable in shape.
- Some engulf invading microbes to defend the body ...
- ... while others produce ANTIBODIES to attack them.
- There's 1 white cell for every 600 red cells!!

PLATELETS are tiny pieces of cell which have no nucleus.
- They clump together when a blood vessel is damaged ...
- ... and form a meshwork of fibres to produce a CLOT.

RED CELLS have no nucleus at all ...
- ... so that they can pack in more HAEMOGLOBIN!
- Haemoglobin carries oxygen in the cell.

## Blood Pressure

This is measured using a SPHYGMOMANOMETER which consists of an inflatable cuff through which a variable pressure can be applied to the arm. A stethoscope is used to listen for the sounds of blood flow as the cuff is deflated to a pressure low enough to allow blood flow. The first set of sounds to be heard indicate the SYSTOLIC PRESSURE i.e. when the ventricles are contracting. As the cuff pressure falls the sound becomes louder then suddenly becomes muffled and disappears. The point at which the sound becomes muffled indicates DIASTOLIC PRESSURE i.e. during relaxation of the ventricles. Typical blood pressure might be $120/80$ mmHg. (the 120mmHg being the systolic pressure; mmHg is the pressure in millimetres of mercury).

ARM CUFF

STETHOSCOPE

mm. Hg

PUMP

SPHYGMOMANOMETER

## Pulse

The arterial pulse is a pressure wave travelling along the thick elastic wall of the arteries, and NOT blood flowing through the arteries. It corresponds with the contraction of the ventricles and can be measured wherever an artery passes close to the surface e.g.

Popliteal pulse in the knee.

Front of foot.

Radial and ulnar pulses in the wrist.

Femoral pulse in the groin.

Carotid pulse in the neck.

## Some Important Definitions

HEART RATE is the number of 'beats' per minute.
i.e. the number of times the ventricles contract each minute. It is usually measured by taking the pulse.

STROKE VOLUME is the 'output per ventricle PER BEAT'.
i.e. the volume in ml. or $cm^3$ pumped out by the ventricles each time they contract.

CARDIAC OUTPUT is the 'output per ventricle PER MINUTE'.
i.e. the volume in ml. or $cm^3$ pumped out by the ventricles every minute.

### CARDIAC OUTPUT = STROKE VOLUME x HEART RATE

As exercise intensity increases, HEART RATE increases. Many athletes MONITOR HEART RATE to establish the appropriate level of TRAINING INTENSITY.

## The Standard Respiratory System Diagram

**RIBS**

**TRACHEA (windpipe)**
This is a large flexible tube surrounded by rings of cartilage to prevent it from collapsing.

**INTERCOSTAL MUSCLES**
These raise and lower the ribs during breathing.

**ALVEOLI**
These are millions of tiny air sacs which make up the lung tissue, and allow gas exchange to occur.

**LUNGS**
These are two elastic sacs which have very thin walls. They consist of millions of alveoli.

**DIAPHRAGM**
This is a muscular 'sheet' which divides the chest cavity from the abdomen and is an important muscle in breathing.

## Gaseous Exchange In The Alveoli

- The bronchi branch into tiny air tubes which end in a cluster of ALVEOLI.
- The alveoli have a massive blood supply in close contact.
- Oxygen and Carbon dioxide are exchanged between the alveoli and the blood.

Carbon dioxide leaves the lungs and is breathed out.

Deoxygenated blood rich in carbon dioxide from the body cells arrives at the alveoli.

Carbon dioxide diffuses into the alveoli from the blood plasma.

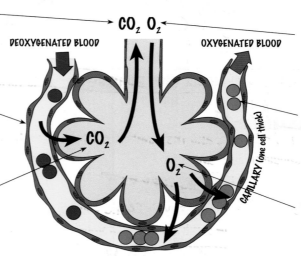

$CO_2$ $O_2$

DEOXYGENATED BLOOD

OXYGENATED BLOOD

$CO_2$

$O_2$

CAPILLARY (one cell thick)

A SINGLE ALVEOLUS AND A CAPILLARY.

Oxygen is continually breathed in to replace that picked up by the red cells.

Oxygenated blood leaves the alveoli carrying oxygen to all the cells of the body.

Oxygen diffuses from the alveoli into the blood and is picked up by the red blood cells.

## A Comparison Of Inhaled Air And Exhaled Air

**INTO THE LUNGS**

OXYGEN 21%

CARBON DIOXIDE (TINY AMOUNT)

WATER VAPOUR (A LITTLE)

NITROGEN 79%

**OUT OF THE LUNGS**

$O_2$ reduced because your body has used some.

$CO_2$ increased because your body produces it

$H_2O$ increased as a by product of aerobic respiration.

$N_2$ a component of air which your body doesn't use or produce so the amount stays the same.

## Breathing

In breathing we first must make the volume of the thorax (chest) larger, in order to breathe in.
Then we make the volume smaller again in order to breathe out ...

**It's the same principle with the SYRINGE and the BELLOWS ...**

RIBS ARE RAISED

DIAPHRAGM FLATTENS AS DIAPHRAGM MUSCLE CONTRACTS

**AN INCREASE IN VOLUME CAUSES A DECREASE IN PRESSURE** - and air enters

RIB CAGE LOWERED

**A DECREASE IN VOLUME CAUSES AN INCREASE IN PRESSURE** - and air is forced out.

**To inhale:**

- The muscles between the ribs contract, pulling the rib cage upwards - a bit like the handle on a bucket.
- At the same time the diaphragm muscles contract causing the diaphragm to flatten.
- These two movements cause an increase in the volume of the thorax ...
- ... and a decrease in pressure which results in atmospheric air entering.

**To exhale:**

- The muscles between the ribs relax allowing them to fall.
- The diaphragm muscles also relax.
- These movements cause a decrease in the volume of the thorax ...
- ... and an increase in pressure resulting in air being forced out.

## Capacity For Exchanging Gases

... depends primarily on the size of a breath, and the number you take per minute.
There are FIVE key terms you should understand ...

| **TIDAL VOLUME** | **RESPIRATORY RATE** | **MINUTE VOLUME** |
|---|---|---|
| • The volume of AIR you inhale or exhale with each breath is called your TIDAL VOLUME. | • How many BREATHS you take in a minute is called your RESPIRATORY RATE. | • The volume of air breathed in (or out!) in one minute is called your MINUTE VOLUME. |

| TIDAL VOLUME | X | RESPIRATORY RATE | = | MINUTE VOLUME |
|---|---|---|---|---|

- This is around 0.5L in adults at rest, but can rise to 3.0L during exercise.
- Between 8 - 15 at rest but can rise to 30+.
- 4 - 6L at rest but can rise to 90+ during extreme exercise.

### VITAL CAPACITY

- Is the <u>MAXIMUM amount of air you can breathe out</u> in a forced exhalation after having a maximum possible inhalation (see the spirometer diagram opposite).

### VO$_2$ MAX

A SPIROMETER can measure tidal volume and vital capacity.

- Is the maximum amount of oxygen your body can make use of in one minute. The fitter you are, the more efficient the alveoli become and the higher your minute volume is. This results in a higher VO$_2$ MAX.

## How Humans Obtain Energy

The Sun is the energy source for nearly every living thing on this planet. The Sun's energy is fixed by plants which form part of our food chain.

THE SUN → GRAIN → CHICKEN → HUMANS →

PHYSICAL ACTIVITY
FEEDING
REPRODUCTION
GROWTH
MAINTENANCE OF TEMP.
EXCRETION
REPAIR OF TISSUES etc. etc.

## Making Energy Available For Physical Activity

• Carbohydrate in the form of starch from foods such as Pasta, bread and potatoes forms most of our immediate energy supply. The starch is digested to glucose molecules which then pass through the walls of the small intestine and into the blood.

SMALL INTESTINE

CARBOHYDRATE

e.g. STARCH

GLUCOSE

BLOOD STREAM

The glucose in the blood is then used in THREE different ways ...

### LIVER

### SKELETAL MUSCLE

### BODY CELLS

• The liver joins the glucose molecules up again to form GLYCOGEN which is stored and subsequently used to maintain blood sugar level.

• The glucose is again converted to GLYCOGEN and stored in skeletal muscle for use in muscular activity. After exercise it is replenished from the blood glucose.

• Glucose diffuses easily into the cells and is used to meet the cell's energy demand via RESPIRATION.

## Maintaining The Balance

The glycogen in the skeletal muscles is used up during exercise, even though glucose constantly enters the muscle cells from the blood. After exercise the muscle glycogen is restored using glucose from the blood. The blood glucose then starts to fall but is immediately topped up from the reservoir in the liver.

## Providing Oxygen To Cells

- The circulatory system carries oxygen from the lungs to all the body cells.
- This oxygen is needed in order to release the energy from glucose in aerobic respiration ...
  ... so that the working cells have enough energy to do their work.
- The rate at which oxygen is delivered to the cells depends on ...
  ... the RATE AT WHICH THE LUNGS CAN ABSORB OXYGEN, ...
  ... and the RATE AT WHICH THE HEART CAN DELIVER IT.

■ = DEOXYGENATED
■ = OXYGENATED

## Aerobic Respiration

... 'is the release of energy from the breakdown of glucose, ...
... by combining it with OXYGEN inside living cells.'

THE EQUATION:

**GLUCOSE + OXYGEN ⟹ CARBON DIOXIDE + WATER + ENERGY**

EXAMPLE: a working muscle cell

GLUCOSE    RED BLOOD CELLS    PLASMA    CAPILLARY

ENERGY

GLUCOSE + OXYGEN ⟶ CARBON DIOXIDE + WATER

MUSCLE CELL

**GLUCOSE and OXYGEN**
These are brought to the respiring cells by the bloodstream.

**CARBON DIOXIDE ...**
... is taken by the blood to the lungs, and breathed out.

**WATER ...**
... passes into the blood and is lost as sweat, moist breath and urine.

**ENERGY ...**
... is used for muscle contraction, metabolism and maintaining temperature.

## Some Facts About Aerobic Respiration

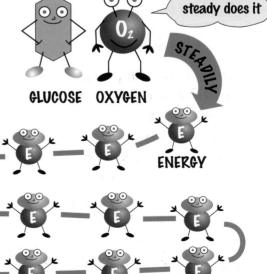

- This is a very efficient method of producing energy, and 1 molecule of glucose can provide twenty times as much energy as ANAEROBIC RESPIRATION (see next page).
- It occurs during normal day to day activity and accounts for our energy production up to about 60% of maximum effort.
- The drawback is that it doesn't produce energy very quickly - only about 1/3rd as quickly as ANAEROBIC.

Nice and steady does it

STEADILY

GLUCOSE    OXYGEN

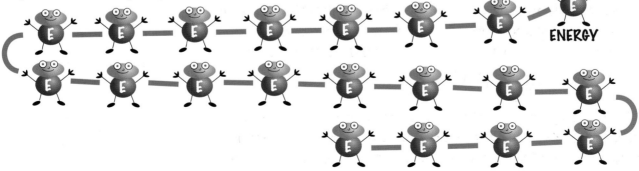

ENERGY

## Anaerobic Respiration

... is the release of a little bit of energy, <u>very quickly</u>, from the INCOMPLETE breakdown of glucose in the ABSENCE OF OXYGEN.

- This happens when the muscles need to work so hard that ...
  ... the lungs and bloodstream can't deliver enough oxygen to respire the available glucose aerobically.

THE EQUATION:  GLUCOSE ⟹ LACTIC ACID + A BIT OF ENERGY

**GLUCOSE ...**
... from the bloodstream AND GLYCOGEN in the muscles.

**LACTIC ACID ...**
... accumulates in the muscles making them feel tired and 'rubbery'.

**A BIT OF ENERGY ...**
... but produced <u>quickly</u> and used for explosive activity.

## Oxygen Debt

- Because the glucose can only be partly broken down in the absence of oxygen ...
  ... LACTIC ACID is produced together with a much smaller amount of energy.
- Build up of lactic acid causes acute fatigue and results in OXYGEN DEBT ...
  ... which must be 'repaid' by continued deep breathing after exercise.

**OXYGEN** to repay debt  +  1/5th of LACTIC ACID  →  **CARBON DIOXIDE** + **WATER** + **ENERGY**

used to convert → Remaining 4/5ths of LACTIC ACID

into → GLUCOSE

GLYCOGEN

FATIGUE is the inability to continue exercise due to:
- LACTIC ACID build up in muscles
- DEPLETION OF GLYCOGEN STORES (in muscles/liver)

## Some Facts About Anaerobic Respiration

- Anaerobic respiration is an inefficient process since it produces only 1/20th as much energy as aerobic respiration (see previous page).
- However it produces energy THREE TIMES faster and so is used during high intensity (explosive) activity over a <u>short period</u>.
- After a relatively short time, the build up of lactic acid affects the performance of the muscles and an OXYGEN DEBT is incurred.

GLUCOSE  EXPLOSIVELY

E
ENERGY
+
LACTIC ACID

The NERVOUS and HORMONAL SYSTEMS allow parts of the body to communicate.

The **BRAIN** is at the centre of the body's communication system.

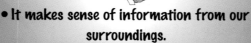

- It makes sense of information from our surroundings.
- It sends instructions to the body.

- The **NERVOUS SYSTEM** allows us to **SEE, HEAR, MOVE** and **FEEL**. It passes information to and from the brain using **ELECTRICAL IMPULSES**.

- The **NERVOUS SYSTEM** is similar to a telephone system.

The Brain is like the handset. It can send and receive information.

The Nerves are like the telephone wire, they are responsible for carrying the signal.

However ...
If there is damage to the nerves the body will not work properly.

The **SPINAL CORD** is the biggest collection of nerves.

Damage to the spinal cord, for example by a broken back, can leave a person paralysed and unable to move muscles in the lower body.

- The **HORMONAL SYSTEM** relies on chemical messengers (hormones) which are released by the brain and other hormone release sites (glands) directly into the bloodstream.

- The **HORMONAL SYSTEM** is an actual delivery system, similar to the postal service.

The hormone is sent from one place and is delivered to another (the target organ) by the bloodstream. When it arrives it stimulates various changes in the body.

Hormones are very powerful chemicals.
They include:

- **ADRENALIN** which prepares the body for action.

  It is released when the body perceives it is under threat, for example, before a game the release of adrenalin increases heart and respiratory rates.

- **INSULIN** which controls blood sugar.

  It is released when your blood sugar level rises. It converts blood sugar to glycogen and stores it in the liver.

The energy we transfer in our bodies comes from the food we eat. It is transferred into many different forms of energy but the two most obvious are MOVEMENT (Kinetic) ENERGY and HEAT ENERGY. Our total energy need is given by the following equation ...

## TOTAL ENERGY NEED = BASAL METABOLIC RATE (BMR) + WORKING ENERGY

### Basal Metabolic Rate

This is the rate of energy transfer which is just sufficient to maintain our body temperature and to keep us alive, but motionless. It is the minimum energy requirement for life and is equivalent to the use of petrol by a car that is quietly ticking over.

R.P.M.
"Ticking Over"

### Working Energy

This is the energy used to go about our daily business whether we are at work or play. The more active we are, the more energy we transfer and therefore the more "fuel" we need in terms of food.

The bigger, or more active a person is, the more energy they will need ... and vice versa. Consequently age is a factor, as is gender i.e. men, being larger, tend to need more energy.

### Energy Balance

Energy is measured in Kilojoules or Kilocalories and it follows that if your ENERGY INTAKE is equal to the energy you transfer then your weight will remain constant. However if this isn't the case, the following may happen ...

## OBESITY

## ANOREXIA

... excess intake of food is stored as FAT eventually causing clinical OBESITY, and resulting in SKELETAL and JOINT problems. Excess body weight can impair performance and can slow you down. The strain on the heart can lead to heart attacks.

... too small an intake of food results in the use of fat reserves and severe weight loss. Ultimately protein is used as fuel resulting in ANOREXIA. Loss of muscle mass results in a less powerful performance. It can even result in death. Anorexia is often caused by a false self-image.

A BALANCED DIET is a very important factor in maintaining good health, and there are SEVEN important components in a balanced diet ...

## The Healthy Heptagon

• These are broken down to glucose to provide fast-release energy.

• These contain lots of energy which can be stored for slow-release energy

• Vitamin A (milk, butter and fish) healthy skin and good night vision.

• Vitamin C (citrus fruits and vegetables) helps to prevent scurvy.

• Vitamin D (milk, fish, eggs and sunshine.) It prevents rickets.

• Provides the 'fabric' for most of the soft tissues. A good protein intake is essential for growth and repair.

• Iron from liver and green vegetables prevents thyroid problems.

• Calcium from milk and cheese produces strong teeth and bones.

CARBOHYDRATE  FATS  VITAMINS  MINERALS  FIBRE  WATER  PROTEIN

• As most of the body is water we need to constantly replace that which is lost in urine, sweat and breathing, by taking in fluids.

• Fibre/roughage is indigestible plant material which gives the gut something to push on, helping to avoid constipation.

## How Much Of Each?

It's not enough to just make sure you eat all 7 of the components above - you have to eat them in the right proportions. Vitamins and minerals are needed in only tiny amounts but the three main components are needed in very definite proportions ...

... although these proportions may change slightly under different circumstances (e.g. bodybuilding, slimming.)

FAT 25-30%
PROTEIN 15-20%
CARBOHYDRATE 55-60%

## Food Sources

### Rules For A Healthy Diet

• Most CARBOHYDRATES should come from fruit and vegetables and some from bread, rice and pasta.

• Most PROTEIN should come from low fat sources such as fish, chicken, lean meat and soya. Dairy produce like cheese and eggs contain a lot of fat.

• Try to include FAT from olive oil and nuts instead of butter and margarine.

• Foods high in FIBRE/ROUGHAGE are fresh fruit and vegetables so include a lot of these in your diet.

• Check nutritional information on food labels.

• Drink lots of WATER especially when exercising.

| Nutritional Info per 100g | |
| --- | --- |
| PROTEIN | 4.1g |
| CARBOHYDRATE | 61.2g |
| FIBRE | 3.2g |

## Special Diets

The ratio of carbohydrate, protein and fat recommended in recent years has been ...

FAT
25-30%

PROTEIN
15-20%

CARBOHYDRATE
55-60%

Although athletes will stick to the general rules for a healthy diet, some may choose to alter the ratio of carbohydrates, proteins and fat depending upon their event ...

### STRENGTH EVENTS

Athletes who rely upon strength for their sport will often do a lot of weight training. In order to help their muscles grow and repair they eat more protein.

> Protein is broken down into amino acids which are then restructured to form muscle protein.

### ENDURANCE EVENTS

Sports people who compete in events which require a high level of endurance will often choose a diet with a higher intake of carbohydrates. This is to provide the energy for long periods of exercise.

> "CARBO LOADING" (This is carbohydrate loading) Endurance athletes may change their diet in this way just before a big event ...
>
> FIRST - They reduce their body carbohydrate stores by eating a diet consisting of protein and fat. This is done for a period of three days, a week before the event.
>
> SECOND - For the next three days leading up to the event, they eat lots of carbohydrate and train lightly. This raises the athletes carbohydrate stores in the form of GLYCOGEN in their muscles. Hence, their muscles can work for longer.

### WATER INTAKE

The most vital component of a competitor's diet is <u>water.</u> When you exercise you lose water through sweat at a much greater rate. This water needs to be replaced in order to avoid dehydration. Drink water BEFORE, DURING and especially AFTER an event. Regular small amounts of water during the event is best.

- Regardless of the type of event in which you compete, you should never introduce something different to your diet, that you haven't used in training.

- The proportions of carbohydrate, protein and fat stated above have been fashionable for the last 20 years. More recent nutritional research has concluded that a more traditional diet, which is slightly higher in protein and lower in carbohydrate is likely to be healthier.

- REMEMBER! Eating FRESH fruit and vegetables is always best because they contain more vitamins and minerals.

Exercise and physical recreation promote general healthiness.
The World Health Organisation defines Health as ...
... "a state of complete PHYSICAL, SOCIAL and MENTAL well-being."

## Physical Well-being

### (a) PHYSICAL FITNESS

- Exercise improves general physical fitness as defined by the 5 S's (It's a bit of a cheat really as Somatotype is used instead of "Body composition!")
- These will be improved to greater or lesser degrees depending on the nature of the exercise. Suppleness, (or flexibility) becomes increasingly important with age and can limit even simple ranges of movement such as tying a lace.

### (b) POSTURE

- Exercise improves your posture by improving your MUSCLE TONE. This enables you to hold your body in such a way that avoids strain on joints.
- This is particularly important for the VERTEBRAL COLUMN. Poor posture can lead to persistant back pain and ultimately time off work (see p44).

## Social Well-being

- Participation in team sports promotes a sense of team spirit and comradeship.
- Taking part in any sport invariably means meeting people ...
  ... who are also interested in the same sport as you!
- Off the field activities are likely to be just as rewarding as the sport itself!
- Also, some sports carry enhanced social status ...

The captain of the school football team.

## Mental Well-being

- Exercise reduces STRESS and relieves TENSION. It makes you feel more generally laid-back!
- Physical recreation can provide mental stimulation if the pursuit is challenging ...
  ... and can increase your self-confidence as you improve.
- You learn to view life in a better perspective.

There are four guiding principles which apply to all fitness training. They are ...

## 1. Specificity

Training must be specific to ...

... the SPORT or ACTIVITY ...

... the TYPE OF FITNESS required ...

... the PARTICULAR MUSCLE GROUPS.

• Marathon runners do mostly ...
... ENDURANCE WORK.

• Swimmers exercise ...
... 'SWIM SPECIFIC' MUSCLES.

## 2. Overload

Training must be raised to a higher level than is normal to create the extra demands to which the body will adapt. This can be done in three ways.

INCREASE THE INTENSITY ...
... by running faster, lifting heavier weights etc.

INCREASE THE FREQUENCY ...
... by training more often, 3 or 4 times a week.

INCREASE THE DURATION ...
... by training longer to prolong the demands.

## 3. Progression

As the body adapts to training it PROGRESSES to a new level of fitness.
Progress to the next level is achieved by a GRADUAL INCREASE IN INTENSITY to CREATE AN OVERLOAD.
A typical graph of LEVEL OF FITNESS against TIME would look like:

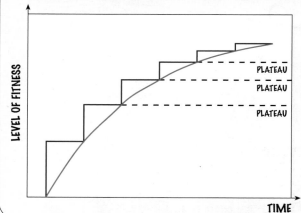

Three important points about the graph.

1. Most progress is made in the early stages.

2. At higher levels of fitness there is less progress.

3. A PLATEAU may be reached where further PROGRESSION to a higher level of fitness is difficult to achieve.

## 4. Reversibility

Training effects are reversible. If exercise is reduced in intensity or stopped altogether then the benefit can be quickly lost. Deterioration sets in after about one week. Strength and speed are gradually lost with muscles losing their tone and size i.e. ATROPHY.

## Muscular Endurance

MUSCULAR ENDURANCE is the ability of MUSCLES to CONTRACT and RELAX REPEATEDLY over a prolonged period of time AGAINST A RESISTANCE.

TWO examples of sports requiring competitors to have muscular endurance are:

CYCLING ...  ... AND ...  ... RUNNING

## Muscular Strength

MUSCULAR STRENGTH is the amount of FORCE MUSCLES are able to EXERT AGAINST A RESISTANCE.
There are THREE types of strength.

### STATIC

- Maximum force versus immovable object.
- Muscle length remains constant.
- Little or no movement of limbs.

Static strength is needed in ...
... TUG OF WAR contest and a RUGBY SCRUM.
Both need to ... hold a steady position
... by maintaining a constant force
... in order to resist an
opposing force.

### EXPLOSIVE

- Maximum force used in one movement ...
  ... i.e. POWER.
- Combination of SPEED and FORCE.

Explosive strength is needed by an athlete in ...
... the HIGH JUMP and SHOT PUT.
Both need ... speed of movement
... maximum muscular effort.

### DYNAMIC

- Repetitive application of force ...
- ... i.e. muscle contractions.
- It is a measure of MUSCULAR ENDURANCE.

Dynamic strength is needed in RUNNING, CYCLING and ROWING.
They all need ... maximum effort initially
... repeated and dynamic muscle action ...
... maintenance of constant speed.

The activities above all need only ONE particular type of strength.
However ... many other activities require TWO OR MORE types of strength in varying degrees.
e.g. Tennis, Rugby, Hockey, Netball.

## Improving Muscular Strength

In order to improve STATIC STRENGTH, EXPLOSIVE STRENGTH and DYNAMIC STRENGTH we must use the FOUR principles of training ...

- 1. SPECIFICITY • 2. OVERLOAD • 3. PROGRESSION • 4. REVERSIBILITY (see p24)

### STATIC STRENGTH
Can be improved by ...
- ... using HEAVY WEIGHTS or HIGH RESISTANCE.
- ... doing a FEW REPETITIONS at a SLOW PACE.
- ... INCREASING THE RESISTANCE.

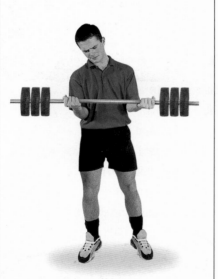

### EXPLOSIVE STRENGTH
Can be improved by ...
- ... using MEDIUM to HEAVY ... ... WEIGHTS or MEDIUM RESISTANCE.
- ... doing FAST REPETITIONS.
- ... INCREASING THE RESISTANCE.

### DYNAMIC STRENGTH
Can be improved by ...
- ... using LIGHT WEIGHTS ... ... or LOW RESISTANCE.
- ... doing MANY REPETITIONS.
- ... INCREASING THE DURATION or NUMBER OF REPETITIONS.

## Tests For Muscular Strength

### TESTING STATIC STRENGTH
- ... DYNAMOMETER ...
  ... which measures hand grip.

### TESTING EXPLOSIVE STRENGTH
- ... VERTICAL JUMP.

### TESTING DYNAMIC STRENGTH
- ... PRESS-UPS or SIT-UPS ...
  ... completed in 1 minute.

## How Speed Is Applied In Physical Activities

SPEED is the TIME TAKEN to move all or parts of the body through a SPECIFIED DISTANCE, for example ...

### FOOTBALL

- Kicking the ball over a long distance, requires good leg speed.
- Chasing the ball.

### CRICKET

- Fast bowling, obviously, but fielding also requires fast arm and torso speed to throw long distances.

### GOLF

- Driving the ball over a long distance requires fast arm and torso speed.

## How Quickly Can The Body Move?

Speed of movement is determined by ...
... how fast the SKELETAL MUSCLES CONTRACT ...
... which is determined by MUSCLE COMPOSITION.

SLOW TWITCH MUSCLES - less powerful, slower contractions.

FAST TWITCH MUSCLES - powerful contractions produced very quickly.

So the more fast twitch fibres you have - the faster you are. The amount of fast twitch fibres the body has is GENETICALLY DETERMINED.

To improve speed you should practice the movement at a faster speed. SPECIFIC SPEED TRAINING will improve how quickly muscles can contract.

## Fitness Test Designed For Testing Speed

**30m Shuttle Run Sprint Test.**

- Starting at point **A** measure a distance of 10m to point **B**.
- The test is to run between points **A** and **B** over this 10m distance until you've covered a distance of 30m.
- Time how long it takes to complete the test, in seconds.

## What Is Flexibility?

FLEXIBILITY is the RANGE OF MOVEMENT around a JOINT. It is also known as MOBILITY or SUPPLENESS. It depends on ...

- The TYPE and STRUCTURE ...
  ... of the joint ...
  ... i.e. bone shape, ligament length.

- The LENGTH and ELASTICITY ...
  ... of the MUSCLES ...
  ... that work the joint.

- REGULAR USE and EXERCISE ...
  ... since joints lose their ...
  ... flexibility rapidly.

It is needed to ...

- PREVENT INJURY ...
  ... as a large range of ...
  ... movement reduces the risk ...
  ... of OVER STRETCHING.

- PREPARE FOR PERFORMANCE ...
  ... to loosen and relax muscles as part of a warm up routine which takes the body through a range of expected movements.

## How Flexibility Enhances Performance

Flexibility is one factor that enhances the performance of a competitor. Improving their flexibility results in competitors being able to ...

### ... INCREASE THE RANGE OVER WHICH MUSCLES APPLY FORCE.

- BIOMECHANICAL EFFICIENCY is improved and performance is enhanced in sports such as ...

... SWIMMING for better stroke efficiency and ...
... SPRINTING for increased stride length.

### ... IMPROVE THE EFFECTIVENESS OF ANTAGONISTIC MUSCLES.

- COORDINATION and AGILITY is improved and performance is enhanced in sports such as ...

... FOOTBALL and HOCKEY for better passing and controlling of the ball.

### ... DISPLAY FLEXIBILITY BY THE EXECUTION OF MOVES AND THE HOLDING OF BALANCED POSITIONS.

- AESTHETIC BODY LINES and AGILITY is improved and moves can be executed with greater form and style in sports such as ...

... GYMNASTICS and DIVING for somersaults, twists, tucks and pikes.

## Interval Training

Interval training involves ALTERNATING between FIXED PERIODS OF EXERCISE and FIXED PERIODS OF REST (or light exercise) for recovery. Careful planning is needed to match the duration and intensity of exercise and recovery with the level of fitness of the individual.

| 25m SPRINT | 30 sec REST | 25m SPRINT | 30 sec REST ... and so on. |

Interval training is effective for most team sports and is an APPROPRIATE method of training for running and swimming.

## Fartlek Training

Fartlek Training is very similar to interval training except that the INTENSITY and TYPE OF EXERCISE ARE VARIED through changes in pace, terrain and style. There are no fixed amounts of each component and a programme can be planned to suit the level of fitness of the individual.

| 10 min JOG | 100m WALK | 50m SPRINT | 2 min REST | 5 min JOG ... and so on. |

Fartlek Training is effective for many sports including running, cycling and swimming.

### EFFECT OF INTERVAL AND FARTLEK TRAINING ON THE BODY

Both have similar effects which depend on the intensity and variation of exercise, but generally ...

- They improve ... AEROBIC AND ANAEROBIC FITNESS
- They increase ... METABOLIC RATE
- They decrease ... BODY FAT %

## Continuous Training

Continuous Training involves LONG, SLOW, DISTANCE EXERCISE (LSD) at a CONSTANT RATE WITHOUT REST. Training at first should be at 60% maximum Heart Rate progressing to 85% maximum Heart Rate as fitness improves and the distance involved increases to beyond competition distance.

### EFFECT OF CONTINUOUS TRAINING ON THE BODY

- It improves ... AEROBIC FITNESS
- It increases ... METABOLIC RATE and decreases ... BODY FAT %

## Pressure Training

Unlike the other training methods, pressure training involves a COMBINATION OF SKILLS AND FITNESS. A skill is continually performed as you become more and more tired. With practice the skill level can be improved with increasing tiredness. A footballer or a basketball player may practice ...

... dribbling and shooting ...

   ... over a set distance, ...

      ... a set number of times, ...

         ... in a set time.

This training is beneficial as it can represent the pressure they can expect to experience in an actual game.

## Seasonal Sport

Many sports take place SEASONALLY and may be classed as SUMMER or WINTER activities.
Hockey, Netball, Rugby, Football, Cricket and Rounders are all examples of seasonal sports.
These activities have a CLOSED or OFF SEASON ...
... for REST and RECUPERATION.

PLAYING SEASON, 30-36 WEEKS

CLOSED SEASON FOR REST AND RECUPERATION, 6-10 WEEKS

OUT OF SEASON, 4-6 WEEKS TRAINING

PRE-SEASON, 4-6 WEEKS TRAINING

- Complete break.
- Recovery from injuries.
- Recreation and relaxation in other sports or activities.

- Light training with gradual build up to a good level of aerobic fitness.
- Light skills training with non-competitive games.

- High intensity interval and weights training.
- Flexibility and 'pressure' skills training.
- Practice matches.

- Playing once or twice a week.
- Maintenance and light weight training.
- Speed work.
- Quality rest and appropriate diet.

## 'All Year Round' Sports

Some sports have become 'ALL YEAR ROUND' activities with specific training requirements. Field and Track Athletes and Tennis players participate in INDOOR and OUTDOOR EVENTS throughout the year, around the world. In order to perform to their maximum potential they need to undergo ...

### ... WARM WEATHER AND ALTITUDE TRAINING

- Elite athletes and players train abroad in warm climates or at altitude to enhance performance. This option depends on funding and financial support being available.

### ... PERIODISATION

- Training programmes are planned to achieve PEAKS at certain times throughout the year.

Long term training causes the body to adapt to the increased load placed upon it by the training. Various parts of the body start to show changes ...

## The Circulatory System

### a) The HEART

• The heart becomes BIGGER and its walls become THICKER (they're muscles remember!).
• The coronary arteries become better at supplying the heart with blood.
• It is able to pump more blood per min ...
• ... and is therefore capable of higher HEART RATE, STROKE VOLUME AND MINUTE VOLUME.
  The heart needs less beats per minute to supply the body with blood when at rest. Resting heart rate is therefore lower when you are fit. Good athletes have resting heart rates of around 50 b.p.m.

The Red Blood Cells

Capilliarisation Of Muscle Tissue

### b) The BLOOD and CIRCULATION

• The number of RED BLOOD CELLS increases to cope with the demands of carrying extra oxygen.
• The capillary networks in muscles start to grow more and more branches and are therefore able to transport more blood.

ALTITUDE TRAINING has this effect on the body, a fact used by many athletes to improve their fitness capacity before important events.

## The Respiratory System

• The diaphragm and intercostal muscles become stronger ...
  ... which increases the maximum lung volume.
  (VITAL CAPACITY INCREASES.)
• This allows greater gas exchange with each breath.
• There is an increase in the size of the capillary networks around the alveoli which means ...
• ... increased blood supply and more efficient gas exchange.

Endurance athletes work hard to specifically improve their circulatory and respiratory systems.

## The Skeletal And Muscle Systems

• The muscles and their associated capillaries become more efficient at exchanging materials (e.g. $CO_2$ and $O_2$).
• The muscle cells themselves use the available oxygen more efficiently ...
  ... which means they can contract for longer and do more work.
• These two facts mean that the $VO_2$ MAX of the body is increased meaning that your body can transfer energy more quickly and is therefore more powerful (power is the rate of transferring energy).
• Muscles may or may not get bigger depending upon the type of training you do (see p.26).
• Tendons, ligaments and bones do get stronger to cope with the increased load ...
  ... and cartilage may increase to cope with impact (particularly in the knees).

Sprinters, throwers and lifters work hard to specifically improve their explosive strength.

## Cardiovascular System

- The heart rate increases with exercise (see p.13).
- ... and the stroke volume increases with severe exercise (see p.13).
- These both increase the cardiac output (see p.13).
- Blood now flows faster and is diverted to the working muscles ...
- ... due to VASODILATION in the vessels leading to the muscles.
- This vasodilation helps to prevent the blood pressure from rising to too high a level.

RESULT:
- THE SYSTEM NOW DELIVERS MORE OXYGEN, ...
- ... AND MORE GLUCOSE TO THE WORKING MUSCLES, ...
- ... AND REMOVES CARBON DIOXIDE FROM THEM MUCH MORE QUICKLY.

## Cardiorespiratory System

- The respiratory rate increases with exercise (see p.15) ...
- ... and the tidal volume increases with exercise (see p.15).
- These both increase the minute volume (see p.15).
- The intercostal muscles and the diaphragm ...
- ... are responsible for these increases.

RESULT:
- OXYGEN FROM THE ATMOSPHERE, AND CARBON DIOXIDE IN THE LUNGS ARE EXCHANGED MORE RAPIDLY. THIS RESULTS IN GREATER (AND FASTER) OXYGENATION OF THE BLOOD.

## Respiration In The Muscle Cells

- Increased muscle contraction means that more energy is needed ...
- ... so respiration in the muscle cells increases (see p.17 and 18), using oxygen and glucose.
- This means that lots more carbon dioxide is produced (and some lactic acid) ...
- ... and because most of the energy produced is wasted as heat, the body starts to warm up and its temperature starts to rise.

RESULT:
- OXYGEN USED UP QUICKLY BY THE CELLS.
- GLUCOSE USED UP QUICKLY BY THE CELLS.
- LOTS OF CARBON DIOXIDE PRODUCED.
- SOME LACTIC ACID PRODUCED. LOTS OF HEAT PRODUCED.

## Cooling Effect Of The Skin

- Blood vessels just beneath the skin open up (VASODILATE) to allow blood to pass close to the surface and lose heat. This causes the skin to flush.
- Sweat is produced by the sweat glands and then evaporates taking heat energy away from the skin.

RESULT:
- VASODILATION OF SKIN CAPILLARIES AND EVAPORATION OF SWEAT CAUSES THE BODY TO LOSE HEAT AND MAINTAIN NORMAL TEMPERATURE.

## The Effects Of Exercise On:

1 A TRAINED ATHLETE: maintains high fitness levels; fine tunes motor skills; enables peak performance

2 AN AVERAGE PERFORMER: maintains health and fitness; facilitates the reaching of higher levels of fitness and performance.

3 AN UNFIT PERFORMER: allows improved levels of fitness and health – rapid at first; lowers resting heart rate and blood pressure; improves sleep patterns and general physical and mental well-being.

## Temperature Regulation

- The CORE TEMPERATURE of the body is maintained at around 37°C due to the ...
  ... monitoring and control of the THERMOREGULATORY CENTRE in the brain.

- BLOOD VESSELS IN SKIN VASODILATE (become wider) CAUSING GREATER HEAT LOSS BY RADIATION.
- SWEAT GLANDS RELEASE SWEAT WHICH CAUSES COOLING, BY EVAPORATION.

- BLOOD VESSELS IN SKIN VASOCONSTRICT (become narrower) REDUCING HEAT LOSS BY RADIATION.
- MUSCLES START TO 'SHIVER' CAUSING HEAT ENERGY TO BE RELEASED VIA RESPIRATION IN CELLS.

GREATER BLOOD FLOW THROUGH SUPERFICIAL CAPILLARIES

SWEAT

SWEAT GLAND

SHUNT VESSEL CLOSED

**IN HOT CONDITIONS**

REDUCED BLOOD FLOW THROUGH SUPERFICIAL CAPILLARIES

SWEATING STOPPED

SWEAT GLAND

SHUNT VESSEL OPEN

**IN COLD CONDITIONS**

## Control Of Water Balance

- Of all the items in the diet, the daily intake of water is the most important.
- Humans can survive for only a few days without water because ...
  ... water makes up 70% of the body's weight and is being continually lost.

GAIN
- FLUID INTAKE
- WATER IN FOOD
- WATER FROM RESPIRATION
3 LITRES/DAY

LOSS
- THROUGH URINE
- THROUGH SKIN
- THROUGH BREATHING
- THROUGH FAECES
3 LITRES/DAY

- The amount of urine produced is adjusted to maintain the water balance ...

- If you have drunk too much you will provide a large quantity of dilute urine.

- If you are dehydrated you will produce a small quantity of concentrated urine.

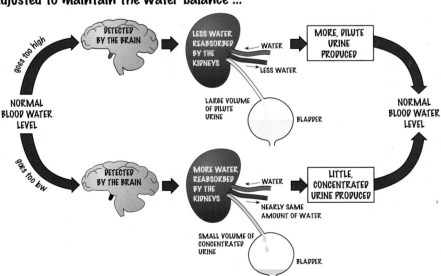

goes too high — DETECTED BY THE BRAIN — LESS WATER REABSORBED BY THE KIDNEYS — WATER / LESS WATER — MORE, DILUTE URINE PRODUCED

NORMAL BLOOD WATER LEVEL

LARGE VOLUME OF DILUTE URINE — BLADDER

NORMAL BLOOD WATER LEVEL

goes too low — DETECTED BY THE BRAIN — MORE WATER REABSORBED BY THE KIDNEYS — WATER / NEARLY SAME AMOUNT OF WATER — LITTLE, CONCENTRATED URINE PRODUCED

SMALL VOLUME OF CONCENTRATED URINE — BLADDER

## The Multi-stage Fitness Test

- The subject runs a distance of 20m, placing his foot over a line marked by a cone at each end.
  The subject must complete each length between the sound of two bleeps. The bleeps come at progressively shorter intervals so the subject must increase their speed, until they can no longer keep pace.
  There are **25** levels to this test.

The test measures your VO$_2$ max. The higher this is the fitter you are.

## The Cooper Test

- The subject warms up, then at the sound of a whistle, he must run around a track for a period of 12 minutes, aiming to run as far as he can.

  At the end of this time the distance travelled is calculated to the nearest 100m.

The test also measures your VO$_2$ max.
The further you run the fitter you are.

## The Harvard Step Test

- The subject records his resting pulse rate. He then steps up and down off a 50cm high step or bench for **5** minutes at a rate of **30** steps per minute. The subject rests for one minute and then takes his pulse for 15 seconds. To find out his score, the subject calculates:

$$\frac{\text{LENGTH OF EXERCISE IN SECONDS} \times 100}{5.5 \times \text{PULSE}}$$

The test measures your cardiovascular fitness.
The higher the score, the fitter you are.

## The Cycle Ergonometer Test

- The subject warms up then pedals for **5** minutes, setting the load according to whether they are male or female.

  The subject's pulse is recorded for 15 seconds, twenty seconds before the time is up.

The lower your active pulse rate is, the fitter you are.

- These **FOUR** tests all measure your aerobic fitness.

- Aerobic fitness is a reflection of how fast your heart and lungs are able to deliver oxygen to your muscles.

- Aerobic fitness is tested to see how an athlete's fitness is improving. Athletes should have a low pulse rate and should be very efficient at getting oxygen to their muscles.

## Agility - The Compass Run

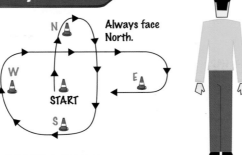

Cones spaced 2m apart.

Always face North.

N W E START S

Starting from the left of the centre cone, run around each cone whilst FACING NORTH AT ALL TIMES. You must circle the centre cone after each shuttle. The clock stops when you have circled the centre cone for the last time.

## Balance - The Stork Stand

The test starts when you have taken position. Hands outstretched, standing on one foot with the other foot on your other knee.

**SHUT YOUR EYES**
Time how long before you lose balance or open your eyes.

Hands held at shoulder height out in front of yourself.

Opposite foot positioned at the side of your standing leg's knee.

Balance on your preferred foot.

## Coordination - Ball Bounce Test

Bounce two tennis balls at the same time

Catch them with your palm facing downwards

This test begins when you start to bounce both tennis balls at the same time.

Continue bouncing the balls as many times as possible without making a mistake.

The test finishes when you make a mistake.

## Reaction Time - Ruler Drop Test

Ask a partner to hold a 30 cm ruler out in front of them. Position your index finger and thumb next to the 0cm mark without actually touching the ruler. Your partner then drops the ruler without giving you any notice.
THE CLOSER TO THE 0cm MARK YOU CAN CATCH THE RULER THE FASTER YOUR REACTION TIME IS.

A partner holds the ruler.

Put your own hand by the 0cm mark without touching the ruler.

## Power - Sergeant Jump

Stand beside a wall and keep your legs and feet flat on the floor. Reach straight above your head. Make a chalk mark at the highest point you can reach.

Jump as high as possible making a second chalk mark at the highest point.

The distance between the two chalk marks gives you a score for your EXPLOSIVE STRENGTH.

## Warming Up

● A warm up prepares the body for the activity it's about to undertake ...

**PHASE 1:** Steady jogging ...  10 MINUTES (approx.)

... warms up the muscles to their "working" temperature, and you start to sweat.

... increases the heart rate, ideally to around 120/140 beats/minute.

... reduces stiffness in joints, allowing greater range of movement.

**PHASE 2:** Stretching ...  10 MINUTES (approx.)

... each stretch should be held for at least 10 seconds.

... your muscles must be warm before you start stretching.

... try to ensure that you stretch each of the relevant muscle groups in turn.

... cold muscles are like cold chewing gum and can snap easily; so be careful. Keep jogging between stretches.

**PHASE 3:** Mental preparation ...

Practice some of the things you're going to be doing when competition begins ...

... passing, receiving, sprint starts and sharp changes of direction may help to prepare your body for the tasks it is about to face.

Give yourself time to think about what you want to achieve. Try to become totally focused and in the right state of mind.

Maintain light jogging and gentle stretching in between the more specific activities.

## Warming Down

This is the transition phase between exercise and rest, and just as you shouldn't go from rest to strenuous activity, neither should you do the opposite. The 3 main reasons for "warming down" are:-

**1** Your heart rate and respiration rate return GENTLY back to normal.

**2** LACTIC ACID and other waste products are removed from your muscles.

**3** It helps to prevent muscle SORENESS and aids recovery.

● Basically do light jogging and gentle stretching of the main muscle groups that you used.

## Sports Shoes

Ideally sports shoes should be designed ...

- ... to PROVIDE SUPPORT to the ARCHES OF THE FEET.

- ... to CUSHION the ANKLE JOINT when impact is made with the ground

  during activities such as running and jumping.

## Basic Rules For Buying Sports Shoes

Forget the hype, forget the style just ...

- ... buy the best you can afford. Remember "Value is a measure of what you get for the price you pay."

- ... make sure they fit properly and can do the job. High back shoes can cause achilles' tendon damage -

  so think on.

## Specialist Sporting Footwear

Different sports nearly all require the participants to wear specialist footwear in order to compete at their best.

Cricketers wear footwear with spikes or rubber soles.

Golfers wear footwear with spikes or rubber soles.

Track runners wear spikes. Road runners wear footwear with rubber soles.

Rugby players and Footballers wear boots with studs.

## Looking After Your Footwear

Unless you've got money to burn you should take good care of all your specialist equipment. Footwear in particular needs some time and effort spent on it if you are to (a) make them last and (b) get the best use out of them. Always allow your footwear to dry naturally. Don't stick them on top of a radiator or in an airing cupboard. If they have got particularly wet, pack them with newspaper to maintain their shape. When they have dried brush them with a stiff brush to remove dirt etc. and then treat them with a suitable application e.g. dubbin, polish, whitener etc. etc.

## Safety Considerations

It is important that **ALL SAFETY CONSIDERATIONS** are observed and applied before, during and after any practical activity.

All practical activities involve risk which can be greatly reduced by the use of common sense and by showing respect for the following considerations.

ALL KIT AND EQUIPMENT IN GOOD CONDITION — APPROPRIATE WARM UP BEFORE ACTIVITY — PLAYING SURFACE IN A GOOD AND SAFE CONDITION — INSTRUCTIONS ARE FOLLOWED — CORRECT TECHNIQUE IS USED — RULES ARE OBEYED

## Considerations Appropriate To Different Activities

### GYMNASTIC ACTIVITIES
- Floor mats in good condition.
- Supervising staff are qualified.
- Use of spotters.
- No overhanging beams.
- Use of magnesium carbonate.
- No jewellery worn & no baggy clothes.
When lifting gymnastic equipment it is important that you keep ...
... your knees bent, ...
... a straight back ...
... and head up.
This will protect your vertebral column.

### GAME ACTIVITIES
- Shin pads
- Face mask/helmet
- Gum shield
- Batting/goalkeeper's gloves ... ... should be worn in appropriate invasion/striking games.
- Goggles.
- Secure net/posts.
- Clear playing area ... ... are needed in appropriate net/wall games.

### ATHLETIC ACTIVITIES
- Well-conditioned, soft landing mats need placing in appropriate jumping areas.
- Rake is removed from pit ... ... before long jump and triple jump.
- Activity in throwing events takes place only when told to do so.
- Use warning sounds to indicate throwing events are taking place.
- No running to collect a thrown javelin.
- Always stay behind the thrower.

### OUTDOOR EDUCATION
- Beware of extreme weather.
- Route Plan
- Take emergency food supplies on long walks/expeditions.
- Check kit with care.
- Ensure someone knows where you are going and when you will be back.

### SWIMMING
- No running on poolside.
- Check depth of water ... ... before going in.
- No jumping in.
- Keep to one's depth.

### DANCE
- Floor mats in good condition.
- Warm up needed ... ... to avoid injury.
- No jewellery worn.
- Appropriate clothing worn.

### OTHER ACTIVITIES
- Follow the rules set by the Governing Body.
- Be aware of potential risks.
- Always be responsible for your own safety.
- Teacher's/Coach's instructions must always be followed.

## Personal Hygiene

Personal hygiene is an essential consideration for any athlete. It helps to keep you healthy. The things to consider are.

The body SWEATS when you exercise, so after exercising you need to wash to remove bacteria and body odour.

A DEODORANT will disguise the smell of body odour, but it won't remove bacteria.

ANTIPERSPIRANTS prevent the body from sweating, and so shouldn't be used before exercise as the body sweats in order to regulate body temperature.

When you exercise LONG HAIR should be tied back to prevent ...
- ... your VISION becoming restricted
- ... your hair being pulled accidentally or deliberately

TEETH which should be clean of course!
May need PROTECTING with a gum SHIELD.
Nails should be kept clean and short to prevent SCRATCHING or becoming DAMAGED.

It is also important to keep CLOTHES CLEAN as they absorb sweat and allow bacteria to breed.

## Footcare

There are two 'classic' foot infections ...

### ATHLETE'S FOOT

This is a fungal growth between the toes. It is found in places that are warm and moist. It causes the skin to crack and peel, making it ITCHY.

- Keep feet CLEAN and DRY.
- Make sure you DRY IN BETWEEN YOUR TOES after showering.
- Use ATHLETE'S FOOT CREAM, SPRAY or TALCUM POWDER, available from the chemist.

### VERRUCAS

These are warts on the feet and are easily spread. They are also hard to get rid of and can be painful. They are caused by a virus.

- Use a VERRUCA SOCK to prevent other people becoming infected.
- Apply OINTMENT to the affected area, available from the chemist.
- In severe cases, a DOCTOR OR CHIROPODIST will FREEZE DRY the VERRUCA off your foot.

### AVOID IN THE FIRST PLACE BY USING FLIP-FLOPS IN COMMUNAL AREAS!

## Tight Shoes

These cause three 'classic' problems ...

CORNS ... these are callouses of thick horny skin that form on joints of toes or balls of feet, where the foot has pressed hard against the shoe.

BLISTERS ... are caused by the foot rubbing against the shoe; which is a particular problem when shoes are new. Break them in carefully.

BUNIONS ... form at the joint between the big toe and the foot when the joint capsule becomes inflamed as a result of pressure from tight shoes.

## Good Posture Means ...

- All parts of the body are well ALIGNED.
- The LEAST STRAIN on muscles, tendons, ligaments and bones at joints.
- Being able to HOLD the body in the correct manner when STILL or MOVING.
- Maintenance of good muscle tone.
- Enabling major internal organs e.g. lungs to function efficiently.
- LOOKING GOOD!!!

## Good Posture Is Achieved By ...

- Flexibility exercises for SUPPLENESS.
- Strength exercises for MUSCLE TONE.
- Standing, sitting, moving correctly i.e. with a STRAIGHT BACK.
- LIFTING and CARRYING objects correctly.

## Poor Posture Means ...

- Part(s) of the body are out of ALIGNMENT.
- MORE STRAIN on and around joints, leading to pain and injury.
- Restricted space for internal organs to function efficiently.
- Muscular Weakness.
- LOOKING SLOPPY!!!

## Poor Posture Can Be Caused By ...

- Uneven muscle development.
- Incorrect or over-exercise of a muscle.
- Standing, sitting, moving incorrectly.
- Incorrect lifting and carrying.
- Lack of balanced exercise.
- Bone or joint defects.
- Tiredness, inappropriate clothing, poor nutrition can also contribute.

## Postural Defects Include

- Abnormal curvature of the spine ⟶ Strained back/abdominal muscles ⟶ permanent deformity.
- Rounded shoulders ⟶ restricted ability to breathe deeply.
- Uneven tilting of the hips ⟶ more strain on one leg, pressure on lower back muscles.

The help given to a casualty before the arrival of proper medical assistance is called FIRST AID. A competent FIRST AIDER can save a life by carrying out some basic procedures.

If a person has fainted, collapsed or been knocked out and is in an UNCONSCIOUS STATE then a first aider should initially carry out the ABC procedure.

A for AIRWAY , B for BREATHING and C for CIRCULATION.

> **HEALTH WARNING**
> ALL FIRST AID PROCEDURES SHOULD ONLY BE CARRIED OUT BY A COMPETENT FIRST AIDER WHO HAS BEEN TRAINED BY A PROPER AUTHORITY e.g. ST. JOHN AMBULANCE.

## ABC Procedure

### A    CLEAR AND OPEN THE AIRWAY

Carefully, using your fingers, remove any vomit, food, dentures, teeth, gum shield or any other obstacle which may be blocking the airway.

- Press the FOREHEAD BACKWARDS ...
    ... and the CHIN UPWARDS.
- This will move the tongue forward ...
    ... and away from the airway.
- The airway should now be fully clear and open.

### B    CHECK THAT THE CASUALTY IS BREATHING

Place the casualty's head in the same position as above.

- LISTEN CAREFULLY for ...
    ... the SOUND OF BREATHING.
- LOOK TO SEE if there is any ...
    ... UPWARD AND DOWNWARD MOVEMENT ...
    ... of the CHEST AND ABDOMEN.

### C    CHECK FOR CIRCULATION

The most reliable method of checking that the heart is circulating blood around the body, is to feel the casualty's neck for a pulse.

- Place two fingers on ...
    ... the HOLLOW BETWEEN the ...
    ... TRACHEA (windpipe) and the NECK MUSCLE ...
    ... and press firmly.
- You should be able to feel the CAROTID PULSE.

## What Happens Next

Make sure that PROPER MEDICAL ASSISTANCE is on its way. If you can't do this yourself get someone else to do it. If the casualty is breathing and has a pulse then the casualty should be placed in the RECOVERY POSITION until proper medical assistance arrives.

If the casualty is placed in the recovery position.
... the AIRWAY WILL REMAIN OPEN
... the TONGUE WILL ALWAYS BE IN A FORWARD POSITION
... any VOMIT WILL SEEP OUT
... the LEGS AND ARMS PROVIDE STABILITY.

**However ...**

If the casualty is NOT BREATHING or HAS NO PULSE then the first aider needs to carry out MOUTH TO MOUTH RESUSCITATION and possibly CARDIAC MASSAGE until the arrival of proper medical assistance.

## Mouth To Mouth Resuscitation

Mouth to mouth resuscitation should be carried out if the casualty has STOPPED BREATHING but STILL HAS A PULSE.

- Open the casualty's mouth wide and squeeze together the nostrils.
- Take a deep breath.

- Put your lips around the casualty's lips and breathe out into the mouth.
- You should notice the chest rise.

- Lift your mouth away.
- You should notice the chest fall.
- Take in another deep breath and repeat the process 12 times in one minute for an adult and 15 times in one minute for a child.
- Check for a pulse.

## What Happens Next

There are three possibilities.

**1** The casualty STARTS TO BREATHE ON THEIR OWN without the need for mouth to mouth resuscitation and they STILL HAVE A PULSE.
Place in the RECOVERY POSITION until PROPER MEDICAL ASSISTANCE ARRIVES.

**2** The casualty DOES NOT START TO BREATHE ON THEIR OWN and they STILL HAVE A PULSE.
Carry on with MOUTH TO MOUTH RESUSCITATION until PROPER MEDICAL ASSISTANCE ARRIVES.

**3** The casualty DOES NOT START TO BREATHE ON THEIR OWN and they NOW HAVE NO PULSE.
The first aider now needs to carry out CARDIAC MASSAGE and MOUTH TO MOUTH RESUSCITATION until the arrival of PROPER MEDICAL ASSISTANCE.

## Cardiac Massage

Cardiac massage should be carried out if the casualty's heart has STOPPED BEATING resulting in NO PULSE BEING FELT. It must be carried out alternately with mouth to mouth resuscitation.

- Locate the massage point. This is just above the meeting point of the breastbone and the rib junction.
- Place the heel of one hand, with the other hand on top, on the massage point.

- With your arms straight press down on the breastbone until it depresses by 4 to 6cm for an adult and 2.5 to 4cm for a child.
- Release the pressure.
- Complete 15 compressions in 10 seconds for an adult and 5 compressions in 3 to 4 seconds for a child.

- Complete 2 mouth to mouth resuscitations for an adult and 1 mouth to mouth resuscitation for a child.
- Carry on by alternating between compressions and breaths.

## What Happens Next

Again there are three possibilities.

❶ The casualty STARTS TO BREATHE ON THEIR OWN and a PULSE CAN BE FELT.
Place in the RECOVERY POSITION until PROPER MEDICAL ASSISTANCE ARRIVES.

❷ The casualty DOES NOT START TO BREATHE ON THEIR OWN BUT a PULSE CAN BE FELT.
Carry on with MOUTH TO MOUTH RESUSCITATION until ...
... the CASUALTY STARTS TO BREATHE ON THEIR OWN or PROPER MEDICAL ASSISTANCE ARRIVES.

❸ The casualty DOES NOT START TO BREATHE ON THEIR OWN and a PULSE CANNOT BE FELT.
Carry on with MOUTH TO MOUTH RESUSCITATION and CARDIAC MASSAGE until PROPER MEDICAL ASSISTANCE ARRIVES.

Sporting activity can put great demands on the body. At times the body is unable to cope and injury results. Some injuries require hospital treatment.

Many injuries however are minor and REST , ICE , COMPRESSION and ELEVATION or R.I.C.E. can be used to ease the pain and tenderness and shorten the time needed to recover.

## R.I.C.E. Treatment

R ... for REST Allow the injury time to recover. Too much too soon ...
... will cause further damage and increase the recovery time.

I ... for ICE Cover the injured part in ice for 10 to 20 minutes. The coldness results ...
... in less blood flowing to the injured part reducing internal bleeding and swelling.

C ... for COMPRESSION Wrap a bandage not too tightly ...
around the injured part to provide support and immobilisation.
This will prevent further damage and reduce the swelling.

E ... for ELEVATION Raise the injured part.
Gravity reduces the amount of fluid collecting in the injured tissue ...
... and also the flow of blood into it.
This will reduce the swelling.

## Suitable Injuries For R.I.C.E. Treatment

### SPRAINS
Injuries to ligaments by wrenching or ...
... tearing around a joint ...
... are called SPRAINS.
They often occur through an ...
... ABRUPT TWISTING MOVEMENT ...
... at the joint.
The area involved will be SWOLLEN , SORE and BRUISED.

If you suspect the sprain is more damaging than you first thought, treat as a fracture and seek proper medical assistance.

### STRAINS
Injuries where a muscle or tendon are ...
... overstretched or pulled with possible tearing ...
... are called STRAINS.
The area involved will be SWOLLEN and SORE ...
... with possibly ACUTE PAIN and LOSS OF MOVEMENT.

If you suspect the strain is more damaging than you first thought, again seek proper medical assistance.

### BRUISING
Most bruises can be treated with ICE ONLY to reduce the swelling and internal bleeding.
However ...
If the bruise is more serious then the R.I.C.E. procedure should be carried out.

## Concussion

Concussion can arise after a person has suffered a head injury. It can lead to loss of memory, dizziness or even unconsciousness.

**What You Should Do**

- Make sure that PROPER MEDICAL ASSISTANCE is on its way.
- Carry out the ABC procedure ...

**A** ... clear and open the airway    **B** ... check that the casualty is breathing    **C** ... check for circulation

- If the casualty becomes unconscious take the relevant action (see pages 45, 46 and 47).

## Fractures

A cracked or broken bone is called a fracture. During the breakage the casualty may well hear a crack. The area involved will be swollen, sore and bruised.

**What You Should Do**

- Make sure that PROPER MEDICAL ASSISTANCE is on its way.
- Do not attempt to move the casualty.
- If medical assistance is imminent make the casualty comfortable and give support to the injured part.
- Otherwise immobilise by fastening the injured part to another part of the body. e.g. If the fracture was to a lower part of the leg then the fractured leg would be immobilised using the other leg.

## Dislocations

The dislodging of a bone or bones at a joint is called a dislocation. The area involved will be swollen, sore and bruised with no mobility at the dislocated joint.

**What You Should Do**

- Make sure that PROPER MEDICAL ASSISTANCE is on its way.
- Place the casualty in a comfortable position.
- Apply no pressure on the dislocated joint.
- However tempting do not attempt to put any bones back in their proper position.

## Torn Knee Cartilage

Knee cartilages can be injured or torn by a knock on the side of the knee or if the knee joint experiences a sharp rotational movement. The area involved will be swollen and sore with the possibility that the knee may lock.

**What You Should Do**

- Send for proper medical assistance and make the casualty comfortable.
- It is possible that the damaged cartilage may well have to be removed.

### STITCH
Piercing pain in the side region of the body. Most likely to occur during exercise.

### CRAMP
Extremely painful muscle seizure. Most likely to occur if you are tired, have been sweating a lot or after vigorous exercise.

### SHOCK
Shock occurs when blood flow around the body is reduced. Can be caused by blood or fluid loss from the body. The skin will look pale, with the pulse getting weaker, followed by erratic behaviour and possibly unconsciousness.

### CUTS AND GRAZES
A cut is the breaking of the skin with the release of blood from damaged blood vessels. A graze is the scraping of the skin. Both can occur during physical contact.

### DEHYDRATION
Loss of water from the body. Most likely to occur during prolonged exercise with the person feeling limp and light-headed.

### HYPOTHERMIA
Occurs when the body temperature is lowered to 35°C or below resulting in shivering. The skin will look pale with a slow pulse. Behaviour may become erratic. Can be caused by being outdoors for too long in the cold and wet. You should wrap casualty in warm clothing and shelter from wind and rain.

### HEAT EXHAUSTION
Occurs when the body temp. is raised to 39°C or above resulting in erratic behaviour. The skin will look pale with a weak pulse. Can be caused by activity in hot, humid conditions when the body can't lose heat fast enough.

### HEAT STROKE
Occurs when the body temp. is raised to extreme levels resulting in erratic behaviour. The skin will look hot with a bold pulse. Can be caused by activity in hot, humid conditions or it may follow heat exhaustion.

The factors can be broadly divided into three main categories ...

## Psychological Factors

- Tension
- Anxiety/stress
- Motivation
- Personality
- Aggression
- Attitude

## Environmental Factors

- Altitude
- Humidity
- Pollution
- Weather
- Large crowd

## Physiological Factors

- Age
- Gender
- Body type
- Skill level
- Illness
- Injury
- Fatigue
- Diet
- Disability
- Lifestyle
- Body chemistry
- Drugs
- Blood doping

Many of these factors are discussed in greater detail on the following pages ...
... or in other sections of the book.

## Environment

### Altitude

The atmosphere is thinner ...
- Less OXYGEN available
- Endurance reduced
- Risk of dehydration

'Thin' air may enhance power/anaerobic events: less 'air resistance' eg. Javelin, Long Jump

### Pollution

Can affect ...
- The Respiratory System: uptake of $O_2$
- The lungs could be irritated by pollutants
- Aerobic/endurance events more difficult

### Weather

Wind, rain, sun, heat, cold can affect ...
- Technique: skill production
- Tactics: short passing in windy conditions

### Humidity

Can affect ...
- Temperature regulation (See p37)
- Dehydration (See p37)

## Pressure/Stress

### Individual
- Alone, no support
- No-one to blame

### With a partner
- Will I let him down?
- Will he let me down?

### Part of a team
- Do I deserve my place?
- Am I doing my job?
- Will I get the blame?

### In front of a crowd
- Will I embarrass myself?
- Too nervous?

### Quality of opposition
- Opponent too good, anxiety, tension
- Not good enough, complacent, over-confident

### Level of competition
- Loss of confidence
- Loss of interest

## Physical Disability

- May be unable to perform skills in the conventional way. Adapt technique.
- Rules may be modified in order for participation.
- Other abilities may compensate eg. wheelchair athletes - upper body strength.

"I am an athlete with a disability, not a disabled athlete."

**Tanni Grey-Thompson**

## Illness/Fatigue

- More likely to make errors.
- Poor levels of concentration.
- Unlikely to perform at one's best!

## Body Shape

Body shape is described by SOMATOTYPING. A SOMATOTYPE uses a 'triangular' graph with 3 axes ranging from 1 to 7 to describe how a person's physique relates to three extremes.

These extremes are ENDOMORPH (fat), MESOMORPH (muscular) and ECTOMORPH (thin). The values for somatotype are always stated in this order. Thus an extreme ectomorph is 117 whilst an extreme endomorph is 711.

**EXTREME (171) MESOMORPH**

Mesomorph
Think **M** for muscles

- Large head
- Broad shoulders
- Strong forearms and thighs
- Narrow hips

EnDomorph
Think **D** for dumpy
and donuts!

EcTomorph
Think **T** for thin

- Fatty upper arms
- Relatively thin wrists
- Wide hips
- Narrow shoulders
- Fatty thighs

- Narrow face and high forehead
- Narrow shoulders
- Thin, narrow chest and abdomen
- Slim hips

**EXTREME (711) ENDOMORPH**     **EXTREME (117) ECTOMORPH**

## Somatotypes Of Performers

All people are a mixture of different proportions of all three types, with characteristics from each extreme. Sports people, however, tend to have strong Mesomorphic characteristics, since muscle plays such a large part in most sports.

Weightlifters
American Footballers
Wrestlers
Sumo Wrestlers also have strong endomorphic traits.

Gymnasts
Sprinters
Rugby League Players
Tennis players
Rugby Union Second Row Forward
High Jumper

Sprint hurdlers have strong mesomorphic body shapes.

Basketball players have Ectomorphic characteristics as well as Mesomorphic.

Somatotype chart showing averages for athletes.

## Gender

After the first eleven years of your life, being a boy or a girl makes a difference in shaping your sporting potential. There are 6 main differences to remember (N.B. These are generalisations) ...

**Strength**  Males have more muscle than females. On average males are 50% stronger. The male hormone testosterone encourages the growth of bone and muscle.

**Cardiovascular Endurance**  Males have larger hearts and lungs, and more blood.

**Bone Structure**  Males tend to have bigger bones which makes them larger and heavier than females. The Female pelvis is wider than the males, for childbirth. The male's more narrow pelvis allows power to be transmitted to the lower body more effectively.

**Speed and Power**  Because males have bigger bones, and more muscle they can move faster and generate more power.

**Flexibility**  Females are more flexible than males.

**Body fat**  Females have more body fat than males.

## Age

You are at your peak fitness in your 20's.

**FORMATIVE YEARS (CHILDHOOD)**
Skill levels develop through variety of experiences, and the ingraining of 'good habits' e.g. regular practice.

"Fitness"

Bones get lighter
Joints get stiffer
Heart rate decreases
Body fat increases
Muscles get weaker
Movements get slower

If you exercise you can slow these processes down and even reverse them.

10   20   30   40   50   60   70   80
Age in years

## Lifestyle

The way you choose to live your life can have serious implications for your performance on the sports field.

Call for a drink on the way home and maybe get a curry.

Out clubbing tonight with the boys!

Good lie in on Sunday morning.

Extra training this afternoon. Practice my heading?

mmm... nice night in tonight with a good book, then early to bed.

Weight training on Sunday morning!

## Personality Of The Performer

Personality is a very complicated subject and there are an infinite number of possible personalities. However, broadly speaking, we can sub-divide people into EXTROVERTS and INTROVERTS.

EXTROVERTS tend to be ...
... chatty, animated, outgoing 'risk takers,' who prefer contact sports and team games involving plenty of action and drama.

INTROVERTS tend to be ...
... shy, deliberate, quiet 'risk assessors,' who prefer non-contact sports and individual games involving strategical thinking and tactics.

It's important to remember that these are just generalisations.

## Getting The Mind-set Right

ANXIETY ... is often caused by fear of UNDER-PERFORMING, particularly if the stakes are high or the crowd is large.

MOTIVATION ... is your real reason for striving so hard. It could be because you want to be the best at your sport or you just might want to make money. It's difficult to succeed without real motivation.

Football Managers experience a full range of emotions!

TENSION ... due to anxiety, causes over-production of adrenaline and possibly nausea together with light-headedness. Actual physical tension can reduce effectiveness of muscles.

ADRENALINE ... is produced by getting psyched-up for your event. It causes increased heart rate, diversion of blood to your muscles and increased breathing ready for 'fight or flight.'

## Aggression

Aggression is defined as behaving in a way that is intended to cause harm to someone else.
The aggression is said to be channelled if it is used in order to achieve a goal.
It may take two forms ...

DIRECT AGGRESSION
Towards an opponent's body e.g. Rugby, Boxing, Wrestling.

INDIRECT AGGRESSION
Channelled through an object (a ball) towards your opponent e.g. Tennis, Cricket.

## An A – Z Of Artificial Aids

**Alcohol**, can induce feelings of well-being and lack of responsibility. It is a form of 'escape.' Unfortunately it can lead to aggression, reduced muscle glycogen, kidney and liver damage and lack of motivation.

**Anabolic Agents** (steroids). These accelerate the growth and repair of muscle, and so are abused to help athletes "bulk-up" for explosive events. This can cause heart and blood pressure problems, excess aggression, male characteristics in females and loss of fertility.

**Beta Blockers** These are taken by performers to help them to relax because they counteract the effect of adrenaline. Used particularly in snooker and darts. Can cause low blood pressure, insomnia, depression and lack of mental 'edge.'

**Blood Doping**. After training at altitude an athlete can remove haemoglobin-rich blood from his body and freeze it prior to re-injection before a competition. The main danger is increased blood density and blockage.

**Diuretics**, increase water loss from the body by urination. In boxing, judo, wrestling and weightlifting, competition is limited by weight category and therefore quick weight loss can be important, but sodium and potassium is lost as well.

**Peptide Hormones, Mimetics and Analogues,** can increase the production of muscle in a similar way to steroids. They can also be used to increase the production of red blood cells to improve oxygen transport. They can cause infertility and blood pressure problems. Most common types are Erythropoietin (EPO) and Human Growth Hormone (h.G.H).

**Narcotic Analgesics** (pain killers). These are used to suppress pain from athletic injuries so that the performer can still compete. Heroin, morphine and codeine are three examples. Invasive pain can lead to worsening of the original injury.

**Stimulants**, make people feel "high" and "up for it." They increase the activity of the cardiovascular system and the central nervous system. After use, a person may feel depressed and listless. Blood pressure may become high.

**Tobacco**, apparently can help people to relax but the price you have to pay is increased heart rate and blood pressure, lowered $O_2$ carrying capacity, blocked coronary arteries, increased risk of cancer, smokers cough, emphysema, bronchitis etc etc.

## Skill

"Skill is acquired ability to bring about a desired result as efficiently as possible with confidence in the eventual outcome." It is learning to do a specific thing with accuracy and efficiency. You know what to do and so you do it, exactly how you want to without wasting any more of your time than necessary. This is being skilful.

**OPEN**  ◄  There are two types of skill  ►  **CLOSED**

What you are going to do may vary. It all depends on your environment.
A Goalkeeper's skill is open. He has to stop the ball from going in the net. The way he does this depends on how the ball is aimed.

You do the same thing over and over again, in exactly the same way. The environment remains the same. A golfer's skill is closed. The skill is repeated in the same way.

### There are **4** ways in which you can practice

**Whole Practice**

This is where you repeat the whole exercise over and over again. For example in an activity which doesn't lend itself to being split into parts, like dribbling a football.

**Variable Practice**

This type of practice is important when learning open skill. It is where you practice the skill in lots of different settings. For example a cricketer plays his shots according to the type and speed of delivery he receives.

**Part Practice**

This is where you break the skill down into separate manageable parts and practice each of the components individually. This is a very common way of learning a skill. For example when serving in tennis you learn how to grip the racket; your stance; how to throw up the ball; and the swing separately.

**Fixed Practice**

This type of practice is used for learning a closed skill. A skill is repeated under the same environmental conditions. For example a golfer will practice his long iron or driver shots repeatedly. The setting of the skill doesn't change.

## Guidance

Guidance is the help you can receive when learning a new skill

You learn how to perform a skill by watching first. This may be a one to one demonstration or you could watch a video or look at a series of pictures. This could give a clear image in the performer's mind of what's required.

A skill may be explained using words, either by your coach or teacher. The explanation could be used to highlight the most important parts of the visual guidance.

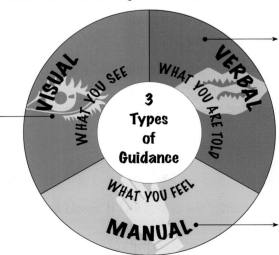

VISUAL — WHAT YOU SEE
VERBAL — WHAT YOU ARE TOLD
MANUAL — WHAT YOU FEEL
**3 Types of Guidance**

You are physically guided or manhandled through the motions of a new skill in order to learn it. You get a feel for what you should be doing. Your muscles can experience what the movement should feel like. This creates **MUSCLE MEMORY**.

## The Feedback Loop

Without feedback you are performing in a 'vacuum.' Feedback allows you to assess your performance and use this assessment to inform your next performance ...

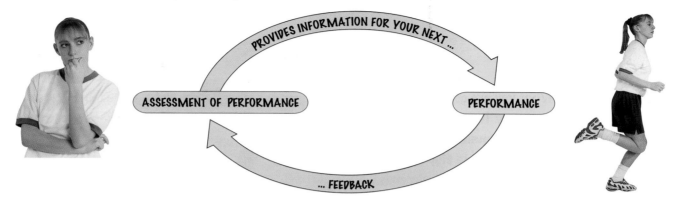

PROVIDES INFORMATION FOR YOUR NEXT ...

ASSESSMENT OF PERFORMANCE

PERFORMANCE

... FEEDBACK

## The Components Of Feedback

There are just two components of feedback ...
... KP and KR ...

**KNOWLEDGE OF PERFORMANCE ...**

... tells you how you performed <u>irrespective of the results</u> and comes from your coach, fellow players, spectators or even video evidence. Not least, you yourself can sense how you did.

**+**

**KNOWLEDGE OF RESULTS ...**

... tells you whether you achieved your particular result <u>irrespective of your performance</u>. Did the ball go for 4? Did you kick the penalty goal? Did you knock your opponent out? Was your serve an ace?

TOTAL **1 6 1**
Wkts **4**
Last Man **6 2**

**ASSESSMENT OF PERFORMANCE**

Correct use of KP and KR will give you an accurate assessment of how you performed and will avoid the possibility of two 'false' outcomes ...

(A) You won but this 'disguises' the fact that you performed badly because the opposition were weak or you fluked it.

(B) You lost and this 'masks' the fact that you performed well because the opposition were strong or they fluked it.

## Using Feedback Effectively

• Feedback should be **FAST** (immediately after the event) and it should be **FOCUSED** (on the key areas for concern), and you need to think about it.

• It should concentrate on **WHAT YOU NEED TO DO** and NOT on what you did wrong. Feedback should be positive.

# TECHNOLOGY IN SPORT

## Effect Of Technology

Technological developments have had an impact on EQUIPMENT and MATERIALS used in sport. This has had an effect on PARTICIPATION and PERFORMANCE in different activities and for different performers.

### Equipment

Use of GRAPHITE or a manmade material such as CARBON TITANIUM FIBRE to make Tennis Rackets or Golf Clubs lighter and more powerful.

### Clothing and Footwear

Clothes have become lightweight, breathable, aerodynamic and more comfortable, keeping the participant cool, dry and able to perform better. Grip fins on some football boots enable the ball to swerve more.

**NEW TECHNOLOGY**

### ICT Information Communication Technology

Records data for analysis of performance. Pressure Sensitive Blocks in Athletics are linked to a timing system and this helps to avoid a sprinter "jumping the gun." Electronic Net Sensors calculate the percentage of first serves in Tennis that are accurate.

### Digital Cameras and Video

Cameras provide an accurate knowledge of performance whose analysis is a component of FEEDBACK. Filming all aspects of the game provides a fuller picture of the individual's or team's performance. Used in a whole range of different sports e.g. Football, Rugby, Athletics and with the advent of underwater cameras, swimming and diving.

---

An example which combines a number of new technologies is a 100m sprint.

- The race can be timed accurately to within 100ths of a second, using ICT.

- Athletes wear aerodynamic clothing and specific footwear.

- An exact and measurable picture taken with a camera aids the decision-making process of which athlete came where.

---

## New Technology And Training Aids

### Heart Rate Monitors

Often in the form of a wrist watch, they can provide exact measurements of HEART RATE. This informs the athlete of training intensity.

### Power Analysis

Currently used by cyclists, there are sensors on the pedals which inform cyclists of how much power is being applied to the pedals. This is likely to be available in running shoes in the future.

*Lonsdale* School Revision Guides

## What It Is And How It Works

Sponsorship is the provision of FINANCIAL or MATERIAL ASSISTANCE by a PRIVATE ENTERPRISE e.g. a company, business. In return it receives PUBLICITY through its association with the sport, the club or the performer.

MONEY/EQUIPMENT/COACHING/FACILITIES/TRAVEL/FOOD

ASSISTANCE IN EXCHANGE FOR PUBLICITY

ADVERTISING/MEDIA COVERAGE/LOGO/GOOD IMAGE

### RECIPIENTS OF SPONSORSHIP

- A SPORT ...
  ... e.g. Amateur Swimming Association
- A TEAM ...
  ... e.g. any Premiership football team
- An EVENT ...
  ... e.g. World Snooker Championship
- A COMPETITION ...
  ... e.g. the Super League (Rugby League)
- An INDIVIDUAL ...
  ... personal contracts with sportswear companies

### TYPES OF SPONSORSHIP

- MONEY ...
  ... for living expenses
- KIT AND EQUIPMENT ...
  ... e.g. sportswear, tennis racquets etc
- TRAVEL ...
  ... e.g. a car
- SCHOLARSHIPS ...
  ... to attend a Centre of Excellence
- FOOD ...
  ... to help with sport-specific diets

MANY OTHER EXAMPLES OF SPONSORSHIP CAN BE FOUND BOTH NATIONALLY AND LOCALLY.

## Negative Effects Of Sponsorship

In return for their investment sponsors expect MAXIMUM MEDIA EXPOSURE. To achieve this they can influence:

### THE DATE, TIME AND PLACE OF AN EVENT

In the 1994 FIFA WORLD CUP - USA matches scheduled to suit TV meant playing in dangerously high temperatures.

### PERSONAL APPEARANCES AFTER AN EVENT

Recipients are expected to attend press conferences after an event, making sure the sponsor's logo is given maximum exposure.

### RULE, LAW AND EVEN SEASON CHANGES

This is done to create greater audience appeal. Cricket now has 'limited over' matches under floodlights. Rugby League has changed to a summer sport in exchange for a huge investment from satellite TV.

## Obtaining Sponsorship

Major sports, individuals, teams and events which are popular and successful easily attract sponsorship. Minority sports, individuals, teams and events that may have less 'public interest' find sponsorship more difficult to attract because they appeal to a smaller audience.

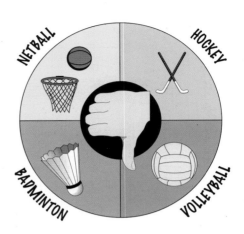

## Advantages And Disadvantages Of Sponsorship

Sponsorship is intended to benefit both the recipient and the sponsor ...
... however there are advantages and disadvantages for both.

  **FOR THE SPORT, INDIVIDUAL, EVENT**

### ADVANTAGES

- AIDS DEVELOPMENT ... of young potential stars
- REDUCES FINANCIAL PRESSURES ...
  ... enabling training and competing to be full time.
- FUNDS EVENTS ...
  ... by covering the organisational and administrational costs.
- PROVISION ...
  ... of coaching, equipment, travel, specialist facilities.
- INCREASED INCOME ...
  ... resulting in superstar salary status.

### DISADVANTAGES

- EXPLOITATION ...
  ... to suit the sponsor's needs.
- LENGTH OF CONTRACT ...
  ... may be short which provides less security.
- SUPPORT MAY BE WITHDRAWN ...
  ... if the sponsor's income becomes reduced.
- MINORITY SPORTS MAY DECLINE ...
  ... as major sports attract most sponsorship.
- WRONG IMAGE PRESENTED ...
  ... through tobacco, alcohol sponsorship.

  £ **FOR THE SPONSOR**

### ADVANTAGES

- SUCCESS, HEALTH, POPULARITY ...
  ... is associated with the sponsor
- MEDIA COVERAGE ...
  ... is a powerful advertising outlet
- LOGOS OR BRAND NAMES ...
  ... become well known and recognised
- OFTEN TAX DEDUCTIBLE ...
  ... can be set against profits to reduce tax

### DISADVANTAGES

- RISK ELEMENT ...
  ... since success in sport is not guaranteed
- MEDIA COVERAGE ...
  ... may reduce or even cease
- WRONG IMAGE PRESENTED ...
  ... with hooliganism at events ...
  ... poor behaviour of individual or team sponsored.

## The Media

The MEDIA keeps us INFORMED, ENTERTAINED and ENLIGHTENED. Sport provides the media with NEWS, EVENTS and SENSATIONALISM which attracts public interest. The different forms of media are constantly growing and changing with advances in TECHNOLOGY and are completely unrecognisable from 50 years ago.

## Types Of Media Coverage

Media coverage is controlled by the people who run it i.e. the MEDIA OWNERS, EDITORS, DIRECTORS, PRODUCERS, REPORTERS, CAMERA OPERATORS. They influence public opinion by the pictures they show and the articles they write.

| MEDIA | AUDIENCE | TYPE OF COVERAGE |
|---|---|---|
| INTERNET | | Fast information access. Possibly educational and/or entertaining. |
| VIDEO/FILM | | Recorded entertainment (best action). Educational (coaching series). |
| BOOKS | | Stories behind events, Biographies - for leisure or education. |
| MAGAZINES | | Specialised or general - informative and educational. |
| RADIO | | Informative and entertaining with results, reports, comments etc. |
| NEWSPAPERS (Tabloid and broadsheet) | | Informative - results, reports, balanced views, opinions etc. Entertaining - sensational stories, private lives exposed. Educational - tips to develop skills, fitness. |
| TELEVISION (Terrestrial - licence fee. Satellite, Cable, Digital, Interactive - all subscription or pay per view) | | Informative - results, reports, comment, text, live action, highlights. Entertaining - live action, highlights, specialised programmes. Educational - documentaries, coaching series, live action, highlights, specific programmes for schools. |

## Effects Of Media Coverage

### THE GOOD,

- Promotes and popularises traditional and new sports.
- Generates finance, e.g. sponsorship, which can be used for junior development.
- Informs, enlightens and instructs.
- Technological innovations have resulted in better coverage, analysis, statistics.
- Raising awareness and interest which results in greater participation.
- Creates feedback for participants, coaches, officials.
- Creates 'star performers' who may become positive role models.
- Ever increasing audiences (worldwide via TV) result in increasing sponsorship.

### THE BAD

- Some sports will go into decline if they receive little media attention.
- Increases the pressure to succeed for participants, managers, coaches, officials.
- Over-exposure leading to audience boredom.
- Exaggerated and sensational stories to attract audiences or consumers.
- Live coverage of events can reduce potential attendance.
- Sports are forced to change schedules, dates, seasons to suit TV or sponsors.

### AND THE UGLY

- Publicises the poor behaviour of some participants, spectators.
- Can create 'win at all cost' attitude, 'gamesmanship', cheating.
- Makes sport 'life-or-death' which intensifies rivalries between supporters.

## In Summary

The MEDIA is BIG BUSINESS and is an ORGANISATION DRIVEN BY PROFIT.
To do this it has STRONG LINKS with ADVERTISING and SPONSORSHIP.

**SPORTS AUDIENCE** Attracts... **MEDIA ATTENTION, ADVERTISING, SPONSORSHIP** Which Results In... **MONEY GENERATED FOR SPORT**

Which Results In... **MONEY GENERATED FOR THE MEDIA, ADVERTISERS AND SPONSORS**

## Good Sporting Behaviour

Sport, ideally, provides both participants and spectators with an emotional outlet for the tensions created by everyday life. Good sporting behaviour should involve controlled aggression against an opponent (or object) within rules or regulations enforced by officials.

PARTICIPANTS

for ...

to produce ...

ATMOSPHERE, SUPPORT and POSITIVE ENCOURAGEMENT

ENTERTAINMENT and DRAMA

who create ...

for ...

SPECTATORS

Good sporting behaviour also involves ETIQUETTE ...
... where a participant shows ...
... RESPECT, HONOUR and COURTESY ...
... for the OPPONENTS and the GAME.

If you should meet with TRIUMPH or DISASTER treat both IMPOSTERS just the same ...

Rudyard Kipling

Examples are:
- Acknowledging opponent's good play.
- 'Walking' in cricket when out.
- Conceding a putt in golf.

## Bad Sporting Behaviour

Bad sporting behaviour by a participant often leads to a spectator response. Spectators may react badly to ...

- Over-aggression i.e. foul play
- Professional foul with a deliberate infringement
- Officials not acting firmly and justly
- Players contesting the rules with officials
- Gamesmanship i.e. 'diving', time wasting
- Unfair tactics i.e. cheating
- Sledging and psyching out of opponent

It has often been assumed that CONTACT SPORTS result in VIOLENT BEHAVIOUR among spectators and NON-CONTACT SPORTS result in NON-VIOLENT BEHAVIOUR among spectators. This assumption as yet has not been proven!!

## Football Hooliganism

For many years there was much debate and concern over crowd behaviour in and around football grounds. Two tragedies, Heysel in 1985 and Hillsborough in 1989, led to a GOVERNMENT ENQUIRY to prevent future tragedies and to combat crowd violence. The result was ...

### ... THE TAYLOR REPORT
Recommendations and other measures included:
- Removal of perimeter fences.
- All seater stadiums.
- Segregation of fans.
- CCTV.
- The sharing of 'intelligence' about trouble makers by different Police forces

## Amateurs, Semi-Professionals And Professionals

People compete in sport as either AMATEURS, SEMI-PROFESSIONALS or PROFESSIONALS. The status of a competitor for a particular sport is defined by set rules laid down by the Governing Body for that sport. In most cases amateurs and professionals do not compete together, although some sports e.g. golf, tennis are 'OPEN'.

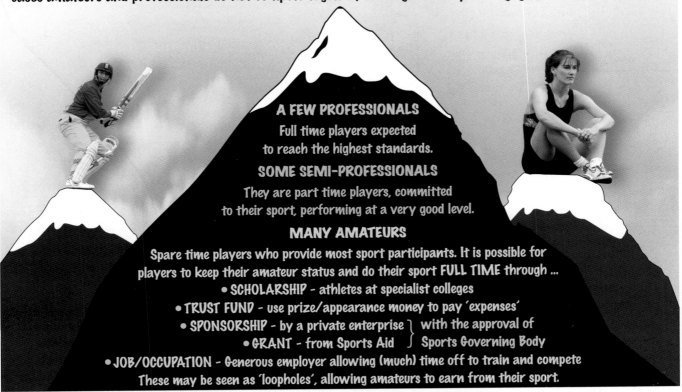

**A FEW PROFESSIONALS**
Full time players expected
to reach the highest standards.

**SOME SEMI-PROFESSIONALS**
They are part time players, committed
to their sport, performing at a very good level.

**MANY AMATEURS**
Spare time players who provide most sport participants. It is possible for
players to keep their amateur status and do their sport FULL TIME through ...
- SCHOLARSHIP - athletes at specialist colleges
- TRUST FUND - use prize/appearance money to pay 'expenses'
- SPONSORSHIP - by a private enterprise } with the approval of
- GRANT - from Sports Aid } Sports Governing Body
- JOB/OCCUPATION - Generous employer allowing (much) time off to train and compete
These may be seen as 'loopholes', allowing amateurs to earn from their sport.

## Traditional Differences Between Amateurs And Professionals

**AMATEURS**
- Receive no FINANCIAL REWARDS i.e. PAYMENTS.
- Play or compete for PLEASURE.
- Originally they were 'Gentlemen' from a HIGHER SOCIAL CLASS with the TIME and MONEY to play sport.

**PROFESSIONALS**
- Receive PAYMENT for PLAYING and COMPETING.
- Play or compete as a CAREER.
- Originally they were 'WORKING CLASS' men with sporting talent who were paid to compensate for time lost from work to play and compete.

## Changing Face Of Athletics And Rugby

Commercial interest in a particular sport increases the amount of money available and the need for amateur status diminishes. Athletics and Rugby Union are two such sports.

**ATHLETICS**
- Olympics and World Class events present commercial opportunities.
- Competitors can receive financial assistance or reward, subject to certain rules ...
  ... e.g. no 'direct' payment
- Amateurism is a concept being phased out at elite level e.g. Grand Prix prizes.

**RUGBY**
- In 1895 rugby became two separate codes.

AMATEUR UNION || 1895 || PROFESSIONAL LEAGUE

- Both attract commercial interest, but only rugby league openly rewards players.
- Increasing International pressure for rugby union to relax its amateur rules.
  In 1995 rugby union became a professional sport.

## Types Of Facility

- These either fall into one of two categories ...

### 1. PURPOSE BUILT
Single or multi-activity.
e.g. Leisure Centres and Clubs

### 2. NATURAL ENVIRONMENT
Hills, Lakes, Rivers Seaside etc.
e.g. National Parks

... or they may be a combination of both.

### PURPOSE BUILT AROUND FEATURES OF NATURAL ENVIRONMENT
e.g. Artificial Ski Slopes, Water Sports Centres, Activity Holiday Centres.

- FACILITIES are built and located to provide a range of challenges.
  Outdoor education centres like PLAS Y BRENIN make the most of the advantages of the natural environment whilst at the same time maximising the challenges for the performer.

## Providers Of Facilities

- They can either be LOCAL or NATIONAL.

### LOCAL PROVIDERS

1. LOCAL AUTHORITIES, TOWN AND PARISH COUNCILS, VOLUNTARY CLUBS, COMMUNITY PARTNERSHIPS, REGIONAL SPORTS COUNCILS. These are run by committees who often employ sport development officers and are non-profit making.

2. PRIVATE ENTERPRISE inc. private clubs, gyms. The commercial leisure/fitness industry exists to look after its members and are profit making.

3. PRIVATE ENTERPRISE OPERATING AUTHORITY-OWNED FACILITIES. It is possible for private companies to run public facilities. They are profit making.

### NATIONAL PROVIDERS

1. SPORT ENGLAND, SPORTS GOVERNING BODIES. These provide centres of excellence for elite athletes and developing talent.

2. VOLUNTARY ORGANISATIONS e.g. NATIONAL TRUST. These provide leisure pursuits and activities for the general public. They are often charities.

3. PRIVATE ENTERPRISE e.g. HOTELS, DAVID LLOYD CENTRES. These exist to cater for private members and to make a profit for shareholders, owners and franchise operations.

## Factors Affecting The Location Of Facilities

- There are many but all you have to do is remember all these 'P's.

PUBLIC ACCESSIBILITY ...
... transport links.

PRICE ...
... cost to build, possible grants and lottery funds.

APPROPRIATE SURROUNDINGS.

**LOCATION**

PUBLIC NEEDS ...
... for families, elite athletes, minority groups.

PLANNING AUTHORISATION
... may depend on environmental impact.

POPULATION ...
... i.e. paying public.

## How A Sports Club Works

A sports club exists ...

... for its members to enjoy participation in PLAYING , SOCIAL and ADMINISTRATION ACTIVITIES.

In return for an annual membership fee or subscription the club should provide:

- FACILITIES - for playing and changing.
- FIXTURES/COMPETITIONS/TOURNAMENTS.
- COACHING - progressing from 'beginner level' to 'representative level.'

These provisions are organised and run by a COMMITTEE OF ELECTED MEMBERS.

A typical committee may consist of ...

### CHAIR PERSON
Highest official who has a controlling vote.

**MEMBERSHIP SECRETARY**
Keeps records of all members and their status.

**CLUB SECRETARY**
Records meetings, distributes information to members.

A calendar of regular meetings will discuss an AGENDA which may include:
- FINANCIAL POSITION
- MAINTENANCE
- ACTIVITIES
- DEVELOPMENT AND PLANNING
- ANY OTHER ISSUES RAISED BY MEMBERS

**FIXTURES SECRETARY**
Arranges matches and venues for all the teams.

**TREASURER**
Manages financial records. Produces current 'balance sheet' showing PROFIT or LOSS.

- ... while SUB-COMMITTEES have the following responsibilities.

SELECTION

TOURNAMENTS

FUND RAISING

COACHING

SOCIAL EVENTS

JUNIORS

## Outside Links With Schools And Communities

Sport's National and Regional Governing Bodies and Local Authorities encourage sports clubs to forge links with SCHOOLS and COMMUNITIES to increase the opportunities for PARTICIPATION and DEVELOPMENT OF TALENT. They do this by providing:

- **FUNDING GRANTS** - to improve facilities.
- **DEVELOPMENT OFFICERS** - who run 'awareness' schemes to attract raw talent and new members.
- **SHARED USE OF FACILITIES** - school pitches, courts, gyms and sports halls.

SPORTS GOVERNING BODIES

ELITE COMPETITOR

SCHOOL AND COMMUNITY

SPORTS CLUBS

## The Main Sources Of Income

Sport requires large amounts of money in order to operate.

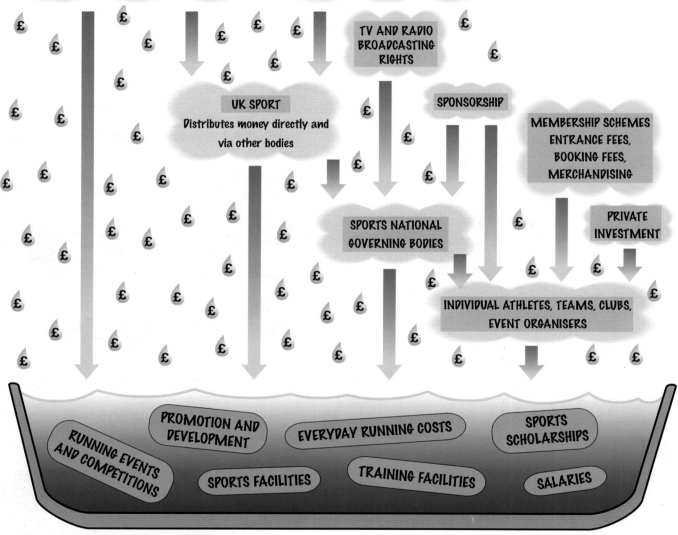

**NATIONAL LOTTERY SPORTS FUND**
Began in 1994. Sport receives 5.6p from every £1 spent. Bids can be made for a lottery funding grant although they must fulfil certain criteria e.g. access for the disabled.

**GOVERNMENT TAXES**
National and Local Government raise money through taxation including gambling levies. Only a small amount of the money raised is given back to sport.

**TV AND RADIO BROADCASTING RIGHTS**

**UK SPORT**
Distributes money directly and via other bodies

**SPONSORSHIP**

**MEMBERSHIP SCHEMES ENTRANCE FEES, BOOKING FEES, MERCHANDISING**

**SPORTS NATIONAL GOVERNING BODIES**

**PRIVATE INVESTMENT**

**INDIVIDUAL ATHLETES, TEAMS, CLUBS, EVENT ORGANISERS**

RUNNING EVENTS AND COMPETITIONS

PROMOTION AND DEVELOPMENT

EVERYDAY RUNNING COSTS

SPORTS SCHOLARSHIPS

SPORTS FACILITIES

TRAINING FACILITIES

SALARIES

## A Typical Example – Rugby

Government Grants, Inc.. Lottery Funds

Sponsorship Deals

Membership Schemes

International Match Tickets

Merchandising, (Replica Kits)

TV/Radio Broadcasting Rights

Redevelopment of Stadiums

Salaries, Players Contracts

Administration

League and Cup Competitions

Promotion and Development in Schools

Training Players, Coaches and Referees

## Major International Events

Major International events e.g. the OLYMPICS, WORLD CUP, WORLD CHAMPIONSHIPS attract worldwide PUBLIC INTEREST. Unfortunately they are often subject to POLITICAL and FINANCIAL PRESSURES.

POLITICAL - Furthering National ideals, Protests, Boycotts.

FINANCIAL - National debt,
Over-commercialisation,
Professionalism.

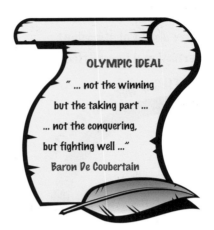

OLYMPIC IDEAL

" ... not the winning
but the taking part ...
... not the conquering,
but fighting well ..."
Baron De Coubertain

## The Summer Olympic Games

The Summer Olympic games is the largest sporting event in the world. It takes place every four years and it is not without its fair share of controversy.

### 1936 – BERLIN

- The games are used by Hitler to further the Nazi cause.
- He refuses to acknowledge the success of black US athlete Jesse Owens.

### 1972 – MUNICH

- Israeli athletes taken hostage by Palestinians.
- The failed rescue attempt results in the deaths of athletes, terrorists and police.

### 1980 – MOSCOW

- Boycott by some Western Nations, led by USA in protest of the USSR invasion of Afghanistan.
- UK athletes ignore government advice and compete.

### 1988 – SEOUL

- Ben Johnson stripped of 100m title and world record after testing positive for drugs.
- Boycott by North Korea.
- Tennis readmitted.

### 1968 – MEXICO CITY

- Black US athletes draw attention to civil rights problems in the USA by giving the 'Black Power' salute.
- South Africa refused admittance.

### 1976 – MONTREAL

- The city incurs huge financial debt.
- Boycott by many Black African countries protesting over New Zealand's rugby association with South Africa.

**-$**

### 1984 – LOS ANGELES

- Boycott by USSR and its allies. Possible retaliation for 1980.
- Funded through sponsorship and TV rights. $235m profit. Some athletes 'paid.' (Amateur status was dropped in 1981).

**+$**

### 1992 – BARCELONA

- Least controversial, a return to (some) Olympic ideals.
- South Africa readmitted and there is a unified German team.

MAJOR INTERNATIONAL COMPETITIONS or EVENTS e.g. Olympics, World Cup, Grand Prix ...

... are arranged by INTERNATIONAL GOVERNING BODIES/ASSOCIATIONS e.g. IOC, FIFA, IAAF ...

... and are AWARDED to a HOST CITY or NATION by INTERNATIONAL COMMITTEES.

## How Hosting Is Decided

A city or country (nation) can make a BID to the international committee and the successful host is announced FIVE years ahead of the event.

The international Committee will judge each bid on ...

**... FACILITIES & INFRASTRUCTURE**
- Venues
- Stadiums
- Accommodation
- Transport and Access (International and local)

**... SECURITY**
of the ...
- Competitors
- Spectators
- Officials
- Dignitaries

**... DEVELOPMENT & PROMOTION**
- Bringing sport to more people
- Encouraging International relations
- Cultural exchange

HOWEVER ...

Hosting an event can be a ...

... A BENEFIT

1984 - LOS ANGELES OLYMPICS
$235m PROFIT

... A BURDEN

1976 - MONTREAL OLYMPICS
$1 billion debt still being
paid off!

## Advantages And Disadvantages Of Hosting An Event

| ADVANTAGES | DISADVANTAGES |
|---|---|
| • INTERNATIONAL STATUS/RECOGNITION<br>Trade is boosted for many years after the event.<br>• IMPROVED FACILITIES AND TRANSPORTATION<br>To benefit the local population after the event.<br>• JOB CREATION<br>Building the facilities and staffing them.<br>• MONEY MAKING<br>Organisers, local businesses and services.<br>• CULTURAL EXCHANGE<br>Tourism is increased. | • DEBT<br>Events are increasingly expensive to organise.<br>• SECURITY<br>High profile events are targets for publicity seeking organisations. This adds to the cost.<br>• INCREASED NUMBER OF VISITORS<br>Puts pressure on local service industries, causing disruption to everyday life.<br>• SPECIALIST FACILITIES - May become 'white elephants'.<br>• MEDIA CRITICISM - They will find something! |

## Sport And Its Value To A Nation

All Governments want to encourage sporting excellence and achievement for their countries, since sport promotes ...

| ... INTERNATIONAL STATUS | ... NATIONAL PRIDE | ... A HEALTHY NATION | ... NATIONAL UNITY | ... SOCIAL INTEGRATION |

Different countries use different approaches to promote sport at all levels.

### UNITED KINGDOM

- Compulsory PE in state schools with some schools SPECIALISING.
- Clubs may have DEVELOPMENT SCHEMES for youth talent.
- Grants, scholarships, sponsorship for POTENTIAL ELITE.
- TRUST FUNDS for some elite competitors.
- SPORT FOR ALL CAMPAIGNS.

### FORMER EASTERN BLOC

USSR, Romania, Poland, East Germany

- Sport was CONTROLLED and ENCOURAGED by the state to produce morale among the workforce and political prestige.
- Sports clubs linked with factories & Armed Forces.
- ELITE COMPETITORS nurtured from early age. They were then 'employed' by the state in industry or armed forces.
- Since 1989 more open professionalism.

### USA

- Compulsory PE in high schools with some schools SPECIALISING.
- School sport is very COMPETITIVE and HIGH PROFILE with much public interest.
- SCHOLARSHIPS to college or university and elite level coaching.
- NATIONWIDE INTEREST in college sport supported with TV and sponsorship money.
- DRAFT SYSTEM into PRO SPORT for top performers.

### THE THIRD WORLD

Developing Nations in Africa (and Asia)

- LITTLE AVAILABLE MONEY means that sport must be CHEAP and POPULAR to develop.
- Athletics and football development are the most rapid.
- ELITE COMPETITORS supported by GOVERNMENT 'JOBS'.
- INTERNATIONAL SUCCESS brings in money!

## Sport In School

Schools encourage participation in sport in a variety of ways such as performer, organiser, coach, captain, official (see MODES OF PARTICIPATION p. 76). This can lead to continued participation into adulthood, especially when links with sport clubs/ leisure centres are established.

Schools promote sport through PE and GAMES as:

### COMPULSORY LESSONS

- National Curriculum (5-16 years)
- Games, both team and individual
- Gymnastics
- Athletics
- Dance
- Swimming

### EXTRA CURRICULAR ACTIVITIES

- Representative teams
- Sport Activity Clubs
- Residential Holidays
- Visits to Leisure centres
- Links with Local Clubs
- Specialist Coaching Clinics

### AWARDS AND EXAMS

- Sport Specific Achievement Awards/Certificates e.g. BAGA, ASA
- Sports Leaders Awards
- GCSE Level Exam
- 'A' Level Exam
- GNVQ

## Activities Available For School Children

These depend on ...

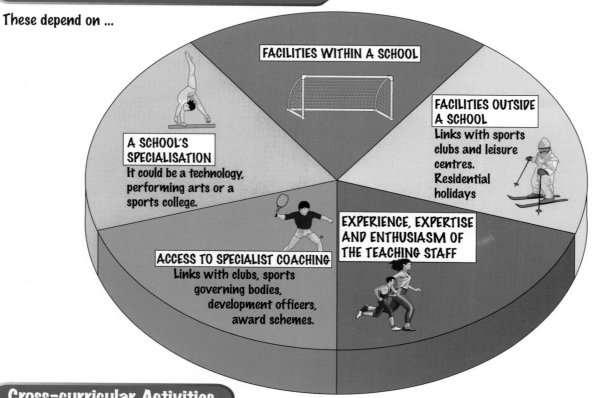

**FACILITIES WITHIN A SCHOOL**

**FACILITIES OUTSIDE A SCHOOL**
Links with sports clubs and leisure centres. Residential holidays

**A SCHOOL'S SPECIALISATION**
It could be a technology, performing arts or a sports college.

**ACCESS TO SPECIALIST COACHING**
Links with clubs, sports governing bodies, development officers, award schemes.

**EXPERIENCE, EXPERTISE AND ENTHUSIASM OF THE TEACHING STAFF**

## Cross-curricular Activities

Schools also promote HEALTH EDUCATION in other lessons across the curriculum in ...

... PSE, SCIENCE, FOOD TECHNOLOGY, DRAMA, ICT (key skills) and HEALTH AWARENESS DAYS.

**CROSS-CURRICULAR**
Diet
Personal Hygiene
Health and Fitness
Drugs Awareness
Social Relationships
**THEMES INCLUDE ...**

## Sport For The Masses

Sport reflects society. As society has evolved and changed in the last one hundred and fifty years so has its attitude towards sport and physical recreation.

Gone are the days where sport was seen as a privilege of the chosen few as today a wide variety of sporting activities are available to everybody.

### Sport for a few in the 19th Century

**MOST ORGANISED SPORT WAS ...**

- ... the privilege of the wealthy upper classes.
- ... seen as a hobby or pastime.
- ... mostly amateur ('Gentlemen').
- ... limited by choice of activity.
- ... not available to most of the lower classes due to widespread poverty.

STATE EDUCATION FOR ALL

RECOGNITION OF THE BENEFITS OF PHYSICAL RECREATION

BETTER WORKING CONDITIONS

BETTER HEALTHCARE

**REASONS FOR EVOLUTION OF SOCIAL CHANGE**

WEALTH MORE EVENLY DISTRIBUTED

COMMERCIAL INVOLVEMENT

EVOLUTION OF PROFESSIONAL SPORT AND ELITISM

TECHNOLOGICAL DEVELOPMENTS IN TRANSPORT AND COMMUNICATION

**TODAY ...**

- ... provision of facilities in schools, communities is better.
- ... physical recreation is promoted for a healthy lifestyle.
- ... amateurism exists mostly at recreational levels.
- ... professionalism has meant improved competition.
- ... there is increased participation in all social groups: women, disabled, juniors, veterans.
- ... there are many career opportunities due to the growth of the sport, fitness and leisure industry.

### Sport for all in the 21st Century

## Women In Sport And Physical Recreation

**OLD TRADITIONAL VIEW WAS THAT ...**

- ... physical activity was masculine.
- ... family responsibilities came first.
- ... physical activity was harmful to the anatomy.
- ... there was a limited range of activities available.
- ... women's sport lacks media attention.
- ... sport is male dominated.

THE SEX DISCRIMINATION ACT EMPHASISED WOMENS RIGHTS.

THE EQUAL OPPORTUNITY ACT HAS REDEFINED THEIR STATUS IN SOCIETY.

**REASONS FOR EVOLUTION OF SOCIAL CHANGE**

MEN ADOPTING MORE DOMESTIC RESPONSIBILITIES

**TODAY ...**

- ... there is a wider range of sporting activities/opportunities available.
- ... barriers to traditional sports are being removed. e.g. football, rugby, cricket.
- ... Womens Sports Foundation has resulted in a greater involvement in administration, coaching, management and the media.
- ... women's sport in the USA is a growth industry!

IMPROVED PROVISION OF FACILITIES e.g. CRÈCHES AT SPORTS CENTRES, WOMEN ONLY SESSIONS.

## The Disabled In Sport And Physical Recreation

Society now focuses on what the disabled CAN DO rather than what they cannot do.
Greater provision for the disabled athlete is made through DISABILITY SPORT ENGLAND (1994). These include:

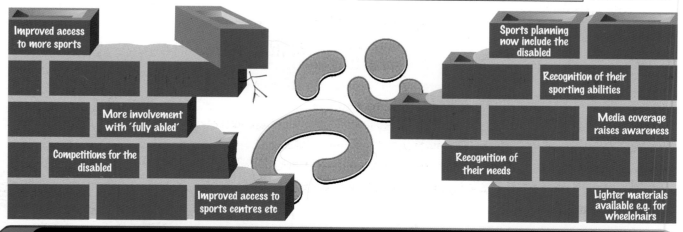

Improved access to more sports

More involvement with 'fully abled'

Competitions for the disabled

Improved access to sports centres etc

Sports planning now include the disabled

Recognition of their sporting abilities

Media coverage raises awareness

Recognition of their needs

Lighter materials available e.g. for wheelchairs

## Encouraging Participation

The government now recognises the benefits of Physical Recreation. Its policy is to encourage greater participation in sport and physical activity. This is achieved through a partnership between:

### LOCAL AUTHORITIES

They encourage participation through ...

... the provision of PUBLIC FACILITIES ...

... the 'DUAL USE' of SCHOOL FACILITIES ...

... and the organisation of 'SPECIAL SESSIONS' at SPORTS CENTRES.

e.g. reduced daytime rates for the unemployed, women only sessions and over 50's sessions.

### GOVERNING BODIES

They encourage participation through ...

... DEVELOPMENT SCHEMES from 'grass roots' through to 'elite' levels, ...

... and UK SPORT and the HOME COUNTRY COUNCILS e.g. SPORT ENGLAND.

UK SPORT

*for all*

LOCAL AUTHORITIES

GOVERNING BODIES OF SPORT

## The Role Of The Sports Councils

UK Sport and the Home Country Councils have many roles (see p.83). One of their roles is to encourage participation at all levels. They do this by IDENTIFYING PROBLEMS and then PRESENTING SOLUTIONS.

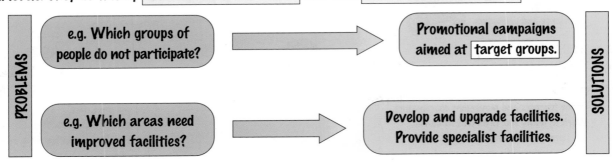

**PROBLEMS**

e.g. Which groups of people do not participate?

e.g. Which areas need improved facilities?

**SOLUTIONS**

Promotional campaigns aimed at target groups.

Develop and upgrade facilities. Provide specialist facilities.

Examples of PROMOTIONAL CAMPAIGNS have been ...

1981 - 'SPORT FOR ALL'-DISABLED PEOPLE

SPORT FOR ALL DISABLED PEOPLE

50+ all to play for

1983 - 50+ 'ALL TO PLAY FOR'

1985 - 13-24 AGE GROUP 'EVER THOUGHT OF SPORT?'

*1991 year of Sport*

1987 - 13-24, 45-49 AGE GROUP WOMEN 'WHAT'S YOUR SPORT?'

WHAT'S YOUR SPORT INFO-POINT

1988 - 'WHAT'S YOUR SPORT?' FOR WOMEN

1989 - WOMEN 'MILK IN ACTION'

1991 - 'YEAR OF SPORT'

Overall there has been a moderate increase in the level of participation. Women's football is one activity where participation is growing as women enjoy greater freedom of choice.

However ... participation in some sports may decline. Snooker and squash are now less fashionable while some activities may be seen as expensive and therefore dependent on individual wealth, e.g. sailing, winter sports (skiing and snowboarding).

## Participation In Sport

Participation in sport or physical recreation is for one of three main reasons...
HEALTH, LEISURE or VOCATIONAL.

A person can participate in many different ways ...

**PLAYER/PERFORMER**
- Recreational, part or full time professional.
- Qualifications? (talent, ability, commitment)

**ADMINISTRATOR/ORGANISER**

- To run the club, organisation.
- Full, part or spare time.
- Chairperson, Accountant, Office staff.
- Professional (business) qualifications required.

**OFFICIAL**
- Referees, judges, umpires, linespersons.
- Full, part or spare time.
- Qualifications and experience required for higher levels.

**GROUNDS MAN/WOMAN**
- Maintenance of sports surfaces.
- Becoming increasingly specialised and technical.
- Qualifications - experience and dedication.

**COACH/INSTRUCTOR/TRAINER**
- Full, part or spare time.
- Work with all levels of ability (beginners to professional).
- Qualifications and experience required for higher levels.

**CHOREOGRAPHER**
- Dance teachers and movement coordinators.
- Work in many sports as well as dance e.g. tennis, ice skating.
- Professional qualifications required.

**PE TEACHER**
- Full and part time.
- Professional and specialist qualifications required: Degree and Coaching awards in a range of activities.

## Other Careers Related To Sport

| **MEDIA** | **SPORTS MEDICINE/ SCIENCE** | **DEVELOPMENT OFFICERS** | **PHYSICAL TRAINING INSTRUCTORS (PTI's)** |
|---|---|---|---|
| • Journalists<br>• Reporters<br>• Broadcasters<br>• Photographers<br>• Technicians | • Physiotherapists<br>• Sports injury clinics<br>• Training method research | • Sports promotion at 'grass roots.' | • Armed Forces<br>• Police<br>• Fire Service |

**LEISURE INDUSTRY**

- Leisure centres employ Managers, Instructors, Lifeguards, Attendants, Activity leaders.
- National parks, Activity centres employ Wardens, Rangers.
- Tourism - activity and adventure holidays employ administrators, leaders.
- Clothing and equipment manufacture and retail.
- Personal Trainers.

PLEASURE DOME

Everyone is subject to FACTORS which may influence their PARTICIPATION in a sport or activity.

## Social Groupings

**FAMILY**
Provide ...
• Early introduction to activities.
• Role models (parent and siblings).
• Encouragement and support.

**GENDER**
• Male participation is higher than female.
• More sports and activities are available to males.

**PEERS**
Friends of similar age or background can be ...
• Active - teams, clubs.
• Non-active who view sport as 'uncool' or a 'waste of time.'

### GROUP PRESSURE
EXERTED BY THESE CAN BE ...

| ... POSITIVE | ... NEGATIVE |
|---|---|
| • Active | • Non-active |
| • Supportive | • Alternative interests |
| • Encouraging | • Expectations too high |
| • High profile | • Too masculine or feminine |
| • Role models | • Cultural differences |

**RACE, TRADITION, CULTURE**
In some countries ...
• 'National sports' are more popular.
• Sport is important and sportsmen/ women have a high profile.
• Women's sport is still disapproved of.

**POPULARITY**
• Football is well promoted, advertised.
• It has high profile role models
• Requires little equipment or organisation at basic level.

**SOCIO-ECONOMIC**
• Unemployment limits participation due to lack of money.
• Some sports are too expensive.
• Local communities or countries may be too poor to provide facilities.

## Other Factors

**AGE**
• Some sports or activities are more appropriate to certain age groups.
• People may participate less and in fewer activities the older they get.

**DISABILITY**
• This may limit the number and type of sports available and who you can participate with.
• Many sports are doing more to provide for disabled athletes.

**ACCESS**
• Depends on how near you live to a sports facility.

**ENVIRONMENT/CLIMATE**
• Top 'winter sports' people tend to come from cold, mountainous regions/environments.

**POLITICS**
• Government involvement on how much is spent on providing facilities for public use.
• The 'Elite' may receive special help to promote excellence and national pride.

**MEDIA**
• Can raise awareness of sports, activities and healthy lifestyles.
• Promote role models.
• Increase the popularity of minority sports.

**EDUCATION**
• A positive school experience may lead to continued participation in later life.
• Compulsory PE in state schools up to 16 years.

## Ladder

| | |
|---|---|
| 1 | A Player |
| 2 | S O Else |
| 3 | B A Newman |
| 4 | A Chance |
| 5 | M R Taylor |

- Usually employed in badminton, tennis and squash clubs enabling players of similar ability to play competitively.

- A player can challenge the player above and if successful take over the higher place.

- In some cases a player can challenge a player up to 3 places above. A successful challenge would result in all the players in between also moving down one place, as the winner takes over the higher place.

## League

- Each team must play a fixture against every other team, usually at 'home' and 'away'.

- Points are awarded for winning eg. 3 pts and for drawing e.g. 1 pt.

- Teams level on points may be separated by 'goal difference'.

- Sports such as Rugby may use the difference between 'points scored' and 'points conceded'.

### ACME B MID-CHESHIRE MOTORWAY LEAGUE

| | | P | W | L | D | F | A | PTS |
|---|---|---|---|---|---|---|---|---|
| 1 | Sandbach | 8 | 7 | 0 | 1 | 24 | 8 | 22 |
| 2 | Middlewich | 8 | 6 | 2 | 0 | 25 | 11 | 18 |
| 3 | Kidsgrove | 8 | 5 | 1 | 2 | 19 | 8 | 17 |
| 4 | Biddulph | 8 | 5 | 2 | 1 | 20 | 9 | 16 |
| 5 | Alsager | 8 | 4 | 2 | 2 | 16 | 13 | 14 |
| 6 | Knutsford | 8 | 4 | 3 | 1 | 14 | 13 | 13 |
| 7 | Northwich | 8 | 4 | 4 | 0 | 17 | 19 | 12 |
| 8 | Sale | 8 | 2 | 1 | 5 | 11 | 12 | 11 |
| 9 | Alderley | 8 | 3 | 3 | 2 | 10 | 14 | 11 |
| 10 | Stockton | 8 | 1 | 5 | 2 | 6 | 17 | 5 |

## Knock Out

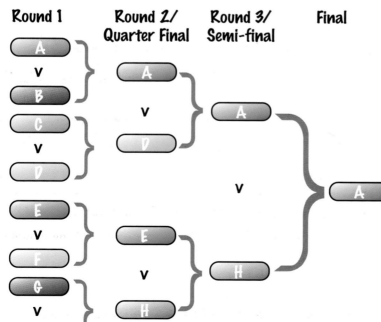

**Round 1** | **Round 2/ Quarter Final** | **Round 3/ Semi-final** | **Final**

- Usually involves a 'draw' to see who plays against whom eg. FA Cup.

- The 'draw' may be 'seeded' to prevent the better players/teams eliminating each other too early in the competition. This should ensure even competition in the latter stages eg. Tennis tournaments.

## Leisure Time

Leisure time is SPARE TIME to spend as you please, away from work and other commitments.

Continuing improvements in TECHNOLOGY has created INCREASED LEISURE TIME for many people.

More MECHANISATION and COMPUTERISATION means ...

### ... AT WORK

- Jobs are becoming ...

  ... less physically demanding.
- More flexible working hours.
- More part-time work.
- More people are taking ...

  ... early retirement.

### ... AT HOME

- Labour saving devices ...

  ... are reducing time spent ...

  ... on domestic chores.
- People can work from home ...

  ... saving on travelling time.
- Home shopping and banking ...

  ... via the TV, telephone and internet.
- Convenience cooking.

## The Leisure Industry

Increased leisure time has led to a growth in the LEISURE INDUSTRY.

Providers of leisure facilities fall into three categories:

### 1. THE PRIVATE SECTOR

- Leisure facilities controlled and run by the Private Sector are many.

  Each one has one purpose only ... to make MONEY! Typical examples are ...

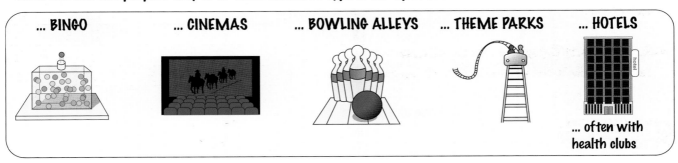

... BINGO          ... CINEMAS          ... BOWLING ALLEYS          ... THEME PARKS          ... HOTELS

... often with health clubs

### 2. LOCAL AUTHORITIES

- Leisure facilities controlled and run by Local Authorities are NON-PROFIT making. Typical examples are ...

... LEISURE CENTRES          ... PARKS          ... GARDENS          ... MUSEUMS          ... SWIMMING POOLS

PLEASURE DOME

Also ...   Local Authority run facilities often have CONCESSIONARY PRICES for the UNEMPLOYED and OLDER PEOPLE during OFF-PEAK times. These groups have more leisure time but less disposable income to spend on leisure activities.

### 3. VOLUNTARY ORGANISATIONS

- These are also NON-PROFIT making. Examples include YOUTH CLUBS, the NATIONAL TRUST and various COMMON INTEREST GROUPS.

The structure of sport must assist and support the DEVELOPMENT of talented INDIVIDUALS, TEAMS and SQUADS from 'GRASS ROOTS' level through to the potential 'ELITE PERFORMER'.

Pyramid levels (top to bottom):
- INTERNATIONAL COMPETITION
- NATIONAL SQUADS AT CENTRES OF EXCELLENCE
- COUNTY OR REGIONAL SQUADS AT REGIONAL CENTRES
- LOCAL CLUBS AND SCHOOLS
- PUBLIC PARKS, PLAYING FIELDS, SPORTS CENTRES

In order to achieve excellence at all levels then good COACHING, FACILITIES and FUNDING are required.

## Coaching

Good quality coaching is vital at all levels to support development. It may be provided by ...

Pyramid levels (top to bottom):
- INDIVIDUAL PERSONAL COACH OR TRAINER
- NATIONAL TOP LEVEL COACHES
- ADVANCED COACHES
- TEACHERS AND CLUB COACHES
- FAMILY AND FRIENDS

UK Sport (formerly the Sports Council) created the NATIONAL COACHING FOUNDATION to co-ordinate and improve coaching for user groups of ALL AGES both individual and team. It involves...

| COACH DEVELOPMENT PROGRAMME | YOUTH SPORT TRUST | CHAMPION COACHING | IMPROVED TECHNICAL SUPPORT |
|---|---|---|---|
| • Introduction to Diploma level qualifications.<br>• Resources and information service.<br>• National Coaching Centres at Universities and Colleges. | • A fun and successful introduction to sport.<br>• Programmes for 4-11 year olds.<br>• 'Bringing Sport to Life for Young People.'<br>• A registered charity. | • Quality Coaching for 11-16 year olds.<br>• Progression from schools to clubs.<br>• Recruitment and development of coaches. | • Personal Coach.<br>• Sports Medicine.<br>• Sports Science. |

## Facilities

There are twelve National Sports Centres in the UK.

These CENTRES OF EXCELLENCE are used...

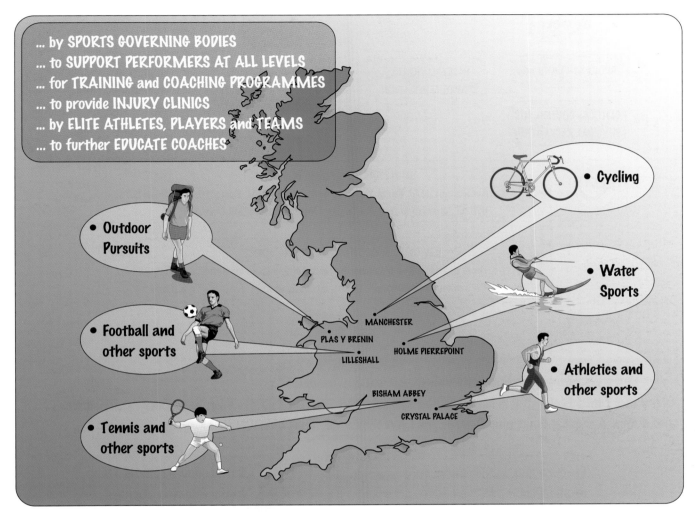

... by SPORTS GOVERNING BODIES
... to SUPPORT PERFORMERS AT ALL LEVELS
... for TRAINING and COACHING PROGRAMMES
... to provide INJURY CLINICS
... by ELITE ATHLETES, PLAYERS and TEAMS
... to further EDUCATE COACHES

● Cycling

● Outdoor Pursuits

● Water Sports

● Football and other sports

MANCHESTER
PLAS Y BRENIN
LILLESHALL
HOLME PIERREPOINT

● Athletics and other sports

BISHAM ABBEY
CRYSTAL PALACE

● Tennis and other sports

The UK Institute of Sport (proposed) will be a NETWORK of facilities based on the Centres of Excellence.

## Funding

SPORTS AID, formerly called Sports Aid Foundation was set up to ...

... DEVELOP EXCELLENCE by helping elite athletes to prepare for and compete in International Events

**Sports**Aid

... ENCOURAGE TALENT by helping disabled athletes and talented youngsters achieve their potential.

It raises money from SPONSORSHIP, LOCAL AUTHORITIES and CHARITIES.
Money is then distributed through GOVERNING BODIES in the form of grants.

HOWEVER

• Many athletes work hard to find their own sponsorship or they fund themselves through part time work. In many cases parents and families often provide financial support.

## The Basic Framework Of Sport In The U.K.

TO DEVELOP and FUNCTION different sports must be part of a National Framework of Sports Organisations, which are effectively STRUCTURED and well MANAGED.
Central to all of this are the NATIONAL GOVERNING BODIES.

- UK SPORT
- SPORT ENGLAND etc.
- CENTRAL COUNCIL FOR PHYSICAL RECREATION
- INTERNATIONAL SPORTS FEDERATION
- INTERNATIONAL OLYMPIC COMMITTEE
- BRITISH OLYMPIC ASSOCIATION

**NATIONAL GOVERNING BODIES**
e.g. Lawn Tennis Association (LTA), Royal Yachting Association (RYA), Rugby Football Union (RFU), Football Association (FA), All England Netball Association (AENA)

**REGIONAL or COUNTY GOVERNING BODIES**
These provide a link between the National Body and local clubs.
They organise regional competitions, squads, coaching courses, centres of excellence.

**LOCAL CLUBS**

## Responsibilities And Duties Of A Governing Body

Every sport in this country is controlled by its own GOVERNING BODY which has many responsibilities and duties. A typical Governing Body is the LAWN TENNIS ASSOCIATION (LTA).

**LAWN TENNIS ASSOCIATION, LTA**

- Encouraging participants at all levels.
- Training referees and umpires.
- Setting down rules and laws, overseeing any changes.
- Developing young TALENT to their full potential e.g. 'Rover Junior Squads'.
- Selecting and preparing National squads e.g. 'Davis' and 'Federation' Cup teams.
- Linking with the International Governing Bodies.
- Distributing funds to local clubs.
- Raising funds through subscriptions, sponsorship, ticket sales, broadcasting rights.
- Arranging competitions at Local and National level e.g. RATINGS TOURNAMENTS which provide scope for a range of challenge for all abilities.
  - All players receive a 'RATING' according to ability.
  - They enter a tournament at the appropriate level.
  - Ratings can go up or down if they win or lose.
  - Funded by sponsorship and entry fees.
- Developing EXCELLENCE by providing facilities, coaching and funding for ELITE players.

## The Sports Councils

UK SPORT (formerly known as the Sports Council) is an organisation which deals with the development of sport and sporting performance in the U.K. as a whole. Each home country also has its own sports council ...

... SPORT ENGLAND, SPORT SCOTLAND, SPORTS COUNCIL FOR WALES and SPORTS COUNCIL FOR N. IRELAND.

UK SPORT and the
HOME COUNTRY COUNCILS

SPORT ENGLAND

The key roles of UK SPORT are to:
- Support elite performers.
- Oversee doping control, ethics and sports science.
- Promote international status by attracting major events e.g. world cups.
- Co-ordinate all organisations within the national framework.

The key roles of the HOME COUNTRY COUNCILS are to:
- Increase participation.
- Improve the number and quality of facilities available.
- Raise standards and develop excellence.
- Allocate Lottery funding.

## Central Council For Physical Recreation

The CENTRAL COUNCIL FOR PHYSICAL RECREATION (CCPR) is an organisation with more than 300 Sports Governing Bodies as its members. Each member belongs to one or more of the following sub-divisions.

| GAMES AND SPORTS | MAJOR SPECTATOR SPORTS | MOVEMENT AND DANCE | OUTDOOR PURSUITS | WATER RECREATION | OTHER INTERESTED ORGANISATIONS |

CCPR

The key roles of CCPR are to:
- Represents its members on appropriate sports councils.
- Promote sport participation.
- Promote campaigns for 'Fair Play in Sport' and against 'Drugs in Sport'.
- Liaise with Central and Local Government, Media, Sponsors.
- Develop award schemes e.g. Community Sports Leaders (16+).

NB The BRITISH SPORTS TRUST was set up by CCPR as a registered charity. It trains people of all ages to be leaders in their community. It does this through a scheme called the SPORTS LEADER AWARDS.

## International Olympic Committee

The INTERNATIONAL OLYMPIC COMMITTEE (IOC) is the supreme power responsible for events connected with the OLYMPIC GAMES. It consists of representatives of Olympic Associations from various countries and the International Sports Federation (ISF).

IOC

The key roles of the IOC are to:
- Select venues i.e. the host cities and plan the games in conjunction with the hosts and ISF.
- Approve the sports to take place in the games.
- Promote sporting ethics e.g. fair play, non-use of drugs.
- Promote sport development and participation around the world.
- Oppose political and commercial abuse.

## British Olympic Association

The BRITISH OLYMPIC ASSOCIATION (BOA) is responsible for events connected with the OLYMPIC GAMES in GREAT BRITAIN.

BOA

The key roles of the BOA are to:
- Choose the British team for the games and organise their preparation and participation.
- Assist with technical and financial support.
- Foster the Olympic ideals and movement.
- Raise money without political involvement.
- Promote participation at all levels.

## Countryside Agency

The COUNTRYSIDE AGENCY (formerly known as the Countryside Commission) is responsible for the ENGLISH COUNTRYSIDE. The other Home countries have their own organisations.

COUNTRYSIDE AGENCY

The key roles of the COUNTRYSIDE AGENCY are to:
- Maintain, conserve and run the National parks e.g. Lake District, North Yorks Moors, Peak District, Dartmoor.
- Give the Government guidance on policy and management.
- Maintain trails, footpaths and free access.
- Promote recreation and understanding.
- Monitor the impact various activities have.